EMU
in perspective

EMU
in perspective

Understanding monetary union

DEBORAH OWEN
and
PETER COLE

FINANCIAL TIMES

PRENTICE HALL

PEARSON EDUCATION LIMITED

Head Office:
Edinburgh Gate
Harlow CM20 2JE
Tel: +44 (0)1279 623623
Fax: +44 (0)1279 431059

London Office:
128 Long Acre, London WC2E 9AN
Tel: +44 (0)171 447 2000
Fax: +44 (0)171 240 5771

———————————

First published in Great Britain 1999

© Pearson Education Limited 1999

The right of Deborah Owen and Peter Cole to be identified
as authors of this work has been asserted by them in accordance
with the Copyright, Designs, and Patents Act 1988.

ISBN 0 273 63302 3

British Library Cataloguing in Publication Data
A CIP catalogue record for this book can be obtained
from the British Library.

1 3 5 7 9 10 8 6 4 2

Typeset by Northern Phototypesetting Co. Ltd, Bolton
Printed and bound in Great Britain by
Biddles Ltd, Guildford & King's Lynn

*The Publishers' policy is to use paper manufactured
from sustainable forests.*

About the Authors

Deborah Owen is an economist who has worked as a financial journalist for *Euromoney* and as a currency strategist for Chemical Bank and Charterhouse Bank. She now publishes her own newsletter on the financial and commodity markets, *The Speculator*, and acts as an economic consultant.

Peter Cole obtained a Master's degree in international economics and was subsequently employed as an economist in the City. After a number of years as a foreign exchange consultant, he moved into fund management and worked as head of department in fixed income investment for various international banks.

To our respective parents

CONTENTS

Foreword by The Rt Hon Sir Leon Brittan QC		ix
Preface		x
Introduction		xi

Part 1 · Political perspective

1	France and Germany: the struggle for political supremacy	3
2	Europe's search for a new order	11
3	The road to the Treaty of Rome	17
4	Development of the European Monetary System	25
5	Fresh impetus towards economic and monetary union	33
6	Political factors resurface	41

Part 2 · Historical perspective

7	Historical perspective	47

Part 3 · Economic perspective

8	The basic criteria for an optimum currency area	65
9	The shifting economic landscape	79
10	Overall evaluation	91

Part 4 · Monetary and fiscal policy under EMU

11	Monetary policy	97
12	Fiscal policy	107

Part 5 · Implementing EMU

13	The euro bloc as an optimum currency area	123
14	Country-by-country analysis	139
15	Prospective EMU entrants	165

Conclusion		175
Bibliography		183
Index		187

FOREWORD

The adoption of the euro by eleven countries of the European Union on 1 January 1999 was a genuinely historic event. The creation of a major new currency, backed by an integrated single market nearly as big as the United States, is an achievement of the greatest economic and political significance, both for Europe and for the wider world. Indeed, the arrival of the euro could well turn out to be the biggest single development on the global monetary scene since the collapse of the Bretton Woods agreement over a quarter of a century ago.

The arrival of the euro will give a new dynamism to the European economy. It will foster the competiveness of European industry, change the face of Europe's financial markets, and act as a powerful and inescapable catalyst for structural economic reform in many Member States. Its presence will very soon be felt, as a practical day-to-day reality, by businesses and consumers right across the EU.

On the wider stage, the euro should become a positive factor for stability in the volatile global system. And over time, as use of the new currency spreads far beyond the frontiers of Europe, it should give the EU a monetary and political voice to match its economic weight.

Yet I have been struck by how little informed public debate there has been in the UK, even now, of the real and momentous significance of this undertaking. All too often, discussion has taken the form of a simplistic and abstract debate about national sovereignty, rather than a careful and balanced consideration of the practical consequences which will affect all of us. That is why I warmly welcome this stimulating and well-argued book. I very much hope that it will make a positive contribution to an essential process of information and education.

The Rt Hon Sir Leon Brittan QC
Vice-President of the European Commission

PREFACE

In order to provide a broad perspective, this book pulls together strands from political, historical and economic writings and we would like to acknowledge our debt to the authors of this material. We have overlaid our own analysis of how economic and monetary union fits in with some of these ideas. In the political section, in particular, a vast topic has been distilled down to what is effectively a thumbnail sketch and to do this we have drawn heavily on a number of works. Special mention should be made of Norman Davies's *Europe: a history*, F. R. Willis's *France, Germany and the New Europe 1945–1962* and D. Urwin's *The Community of Europe*.

We are grateful to The Economist Intelligence Unit for permission to reproduce an extract from their publication. Thanks are also due to Datastream/ICV and Oxford University Press for permission to use some of their data. The International Monetary Fund (IMF) and the Organisation for Economic Co-operation and Development (OECD) have also been a useful source of economic data.

Finally we would like to thank Richard Stagg and Elizabeth Truran of Financial Times Prentice Hall for their help and encouragement.

INTRODUCTION

Europe has chosen to mark the new millennium by embarking on an ambitious plan to forge a monetary alliance between a broad spread of countries. Economic and Monetary Union (EMU) has created a new global economic bloc of almost the same size as the US which, if successful, will come to be viewed as the most significant achievement at the turning point of the millennium. Failure has not been contemplated – there is no provision either for an individual country to withdraw or for the system as a whole to be dismantled. Yet a number of economists question its viability. Should they prove to be correct, the collapse of EMU would be a financial Armaggedon.

In this book we explore the dynamics of monetary union. *EMU in Perspective* is not a checklist for euro preparedness; it aims to provide a deeper insight and understanding into this vast economic experiment that will enable the reader to evaluate how it is progressing and hence reach better informed decisions.

This historic development is *the* issue of our time; it affects the everyday lives of not only all those people living in the participating countries but also anyone who does business or even holidays in these countries. Given its potential impact, EMU has elicited remarkably little interest from the European electorate. There is very little comprehension about its full import for both the European community and the world at large. This indifference is not altogether surprising. The path towards monetary union has been a long and extremely winding one with many a setback along the way. For many years it had seemed to be no more than a far-off pipedream of Europe's political élite. And then suddenly – almost from nowhere – it has become the here and now.

Very few businesses are fully prepared to meet both the challenges and the opportunities that EMU will present. Many people both within Europe and outside it are still perplexed by the concept of EMU and its underlying rationale. Is it really worth such enormous financial upheaval just to save on a few transaction costs? What are the chances of its surviving? And is monetary union just a staging post towards full political union? To add to the confusion, the debate about EMU has tended to polarize into two very distinct camps: those that passionately support the idea and those that are equally vehemently opposed to it.

EMU is the result of a complex interweaving of political and economic factors. It is impossible to understand the rationale for the project or to evaluate its chances of success without first standing back and looking at it from a broad perspective. This book aims to provide that perspective from three different angles: political, economic and historical. It has been written for people in businesses and financial institutions, students and indeed anyone whose work brings them into contact with the eurozone.

POLITICAL PERSPECTIVE

Although economic matters have come to dominate the European agenda, a union of European countries was originally conceived as an answer to the continent's political rather than economic problems. Part 1 looks at this political dimension.

The present efforts to integrate Europe into a more cohesive group of countries have their roots in the latter part of the nineteenth century when the newly formed German state began to challenge France's hegemony. Chapter 1 traces this struggle. It is, perforce, rather a whistlestop tour of such a vast topic, but for those unfamiliar with this period of European history, it is important to have a background appreciation of how the deep-rooted animosity between France and Germany was such a flashpoint in European relations. The years of enmity and war reached their nadir with the Second World War. The destruction and suffering engendered by this event brought with it a realization that a new era had to be created in European relations. To no one was this more evident than Winston Churchill and in 1946 he called for the formation of 'a kind of United States of Europe' (Gilbert, 1988).

Trying to foster closer relations between countries traumatized by the events of the Second World War was, however, no easy matter and Chapters 2 to 5 look at the struggle to achieve a community of European nations. The first breakthrough came with the establishment of the European Coal and Steel Community agreement. The experience of these first steps towards integration was important in shaping the decision that economic policy should spearhead the drive towards achieving a better understanding between the European nations. However, after the setting-up of the European Economic Community (EEC) in 1957, there followed a period of almost two decades when the concept of closer co-operation languished in the doldrums as first de Gaulle blocked the UK's membership and then a series of economic shocks forced governments to focus on their domestic problems. The European movement was regalvanized in the 1980s with the introduction of the Single European Act of 1985. This was followed up three years later by the Delors Report which laid out a step-by-step plan for achieving monetary and economic union. In 1992 these proposals were embodied in the Maastricht Treaty. European political geometry took on an entirely new dimension in 1989 with the collapse of communism and Chapter 6 analyzes the implications that this had for the European Union (EU).

HISTORICAL PERSPECTIVE

The strong political undercurrent behind the drive to establish a closer economic association between European countries has raised the question of whether EMU is just a staging post along the road to full political union. In this respect, it is interesting to look at the experience of other monetary unions. Although none of the previous currency unions has been on the same scale as that currently being embarked upon in Europe, there are nevertheless some interesting lessons to be learnt from studying these historical precedents. Part 2 of the book examines EMU from this historical perspective. In some cases, such as Germany and Italy in the mid-nineteenth century, the monetary union followed on after political union (although, pre-unification, the individual German states had formed a customs union, the *Zollverein*). Currency unions such as the Latin Monetary Union, which have not been accompanied by political integration, have had a much more chequered history. Based on this historical experience, if the present construction of EMU does run into difficulties, serious consideration will no doubt be given to pressing ahead with closer political union.

ECONOMIC PERSPECTIVE

The Maastricht Treaty not only laid down the ground rules for EMU but it also established a list of economic conditions that prospective countries must satisfy before they could become part of the union. Economists have developed some conclusions about what type of economies are best suited to forming currency unions: these are known collectively as the theory of optimum currency areas. Essentially this theory weighs up the advantages and disadvantages of a country forming a monetary union by looking at whether its factors of production (the most important of which is labour) are mobile; whether the economy concerned is 'open' (i.e., external trade constitutes a significant proportion of overall GDP) and whether it is broadly in synchronization with other countries in the area. Curiously, in laying down the criteria that would decide which countries would be eligible to become part of the eurozone, the authorities do not seem to have paid much attention to this theory. Part 3 of the book explains the main tenets of the theory of optimum currency areas and its implications for EMU.

MONETARY AND FISCAL POLICY UNDER EMU

An assessment of the prospects and future implications of economic and monetary union cannot be undertaken without first understanding how it operates. In Part 4 therefore we have explained, in fairly simple terms, how monetary and fiscal policy works under the new regime and some of the problems that will need to be addressed. Clearly the major question is, with the European Central Bank now responsible for setting the rate of interest on the euro, will it prove possible to keep the economic temperature across such a broad spread of countries roughly the same – especially as monetary changes affect countries to differing degrees? Having assigned monetary policy to a centralized body, individual governments now have to rely entirely on fiscal policy to temper any economic irregularities. In order to try and minimize the scope for a mismatch between centralized monetary and decentralized fiscal policy, a stabilization pact has been introduced which sets a limit on government budget deficits of 3 per cent of GDP. There is concern, however, that this ceiling may be too restrictive and that it will hamper governments' ability to cushion cyclical downturns.

IMPLEMENTING EMU

After having looked at the underlying political and economic rationale for EMU and the mechanics of monetary and fiscal policy, we are now in a position to look at how easy it will be actually to implement economic and monetary union. Part 5 looks at how Europe fits into the theoretical precepts of what an optimum currency area should be. A country-by-country analysis of the founding members of the eurozone assesses which economies are likely to adapt successfully to EMU and which are likely to experience more difficulty. This section also looks at the structure of the four members of the EU which, for various reasons, have decided not to embark on the first wave of EMU.

CONCLUSION

Lastly, we have pulled all these threads together and drawn some tentative conclusions about where the pressure points are likely to occur. It should be stressed, however, that it is not the purpose of this book to make a hard and fast case either for or against EMU. Nothing quite like this has happened before and we are, therefore, in uncharted waters. It is also an evolving situation: governments will, presumably, act to try and reduce some of the structural rigidities that are likely to impede EMU's smooth functioning. The policy decisions necessary to establish this effective operating framework are likely to be the subject of fierce national debates. EMU is also likely to remain a contentious issue in countries which might join the second wave of entrants. Trying to second-guess the outcome of a myriad of different factors is a rather fruitless task and one that is inevitably prone to a wide margin of error. Instead, we hope that by elucidating some of the background issues we will provide readers with the tools by which they themselves will be able to engage in the EMU debate and evaluate its ongoing progress.

POLITICAL
PERSPECTIVE

The drive towards forging an integrated Europe in the 1990s has focused almost exclusively on economic policy, with the Maastricht treaty, in effect, acting as the north pole of the European compass. Thousands of column-inches have been devoted to scrutinizing the fine print of this treaty and analyzing its macro-economic implications. But, in order to appreciate fully the policy of Economic and Monetary Union (EMU), it is necessary to set it within the much broader political context of Franco-German relations.

....

Chapter 1

FRANCE AND GERMANY: THE STRUGGLE FOR POLITICAL SUPREMACY

The industrial revolution in the nineteenth century gave Germany a military advantage over France and it was not long before this superior power was being exercised. The Franco-Prussian war of 1870–1 sparked off a bitter enmity between the two countries that was to last for 75 years and give rise to two world wars. Not surprisingly, the experience of these events played a major part in shaping political developments in Europe in the latter part of the twentieth century.

THE INDUSTRIAL REVOLUTION HERALDS A NEW ERA IN EUROPE

To trace the start of the long-standing feud between France and Germany we really need to go back to the 1870s when Europe entered a new era with the formation of a united Germany and a united Italy. It is important to bear in mind that, at this time, there was no over-arching international organization like the United Nations to which questions of border disputes could be referred. Individual states existed by dint of being able to defend themselves from aggressors. Peace was therefore achieved through a balance of power between the Great Powers; smaller countries retained their independence through a series of treaties with their larger neigh-

3

bours. In the latter part of the nineteenth century this balance of power was, however, thrown out of equilibrium by the growing industrialization that unleashed a ferment of socio-economic changes.

Across Europe, the new economic dynamism generated an explosive rise in the output of coal and iron, thousands of kilometres of railway line were laid down and there was a huge migration of people from the countryside to the towns. The new technology also made it easier to travel and colonize new areas of the world.

A SHIFT IN THE BALANCE OF POWER

Until the latter part of the nineteenth century, the determining factor in a country's ability to wage war successfully was the size of its population but, with the onset of the industrial revolution, the yardstick shifted to industrial capability. In this respect, Germany had an enormous advantage. It was not long before its huge reserves of mineral resources, harnessed to the developing industrial technology, made the newly created state the powerhouse of Europe. By 1900 German coal production dwarfed that of France and was rapidly catching up with that of Britain (*see* Fig. 1.1).

FRANCO-PRUSSIAN WAR

The first real proof of Germany's superior might was the Franco-Prussian war of 1870–1. For much of the nineteenth century France was regarded as the major military threat in Europe but first at Metz and then at Sedan French troops were ignominiously defeated by a coalition of the German states. Paris was besieged during the winter months of 1870 and was eventually forced to surrender formally on 28 January 1871. The starvation conditions endured by the inhabitants left an indelible scar that was to return and haunt them 70 years later. At the Treaty of Frankfurt, signed on 10 May

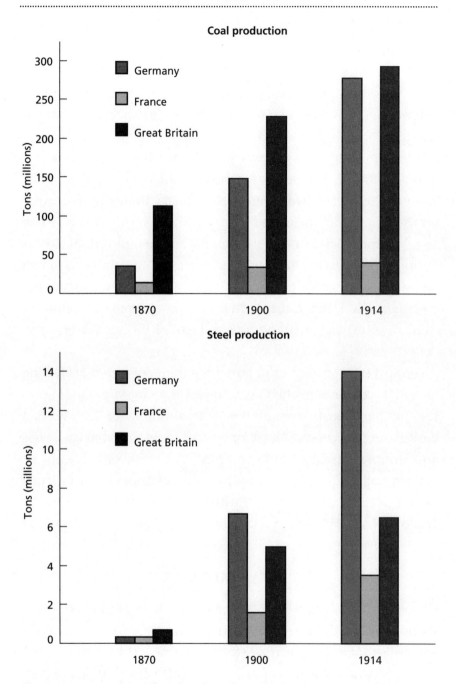

Fig. 1.1 A comparison of coal and steel production in Germany, France and Great Britain between 1870 and 1914
Source: Taylor, 1971, pp. xxix and xxx

1871, the French were forced to cede Alsace and Lorraine and to pay an indemnity of 5 billion francs (Taylor, 1971).

The war was a watershed in relations between the two countries; not only did it effectively mark the end of French hegemony in Europe but it was also the start of the long-running Franco-German enmity.

After the Franco-Prussian war there then followed a long period of peace. One of the reasons for the lack of conflict within Europe was that the Great Powers were preoccupied with the race to scoop up the remaining unclaimed corners of the world. This was one area in which Germany lagged behind France and Britain. It was during a speech to the Reichstag in December 1897 that Count von Bülow made his now famous demand for Germany to have her place in the sun. But, rather than try to colonize remote countries, Germany's expansionary ambitions focused on her Eastern borders.

Beneath the apparent calm post-1870 there was a general feeling of restlessness and all the Great Powers were rapidly building up their military capabilities. By the 1900s a number of disputes had broken out between the Great Powers over their colonial territories and trouble was beginning to erupt in the Balkans. Teams of nations had been already been drawn up as a result of the Triple Alliance (1882) of Germany, Austria-Hungary and Italy and the Triple Entente (1907) of France, Britain and Russia.

FIRST WORLD WAR

Historians have debated endlessly over the exact causes of the First World War but the fatal spark was the assassination of Archduke Francis-Ferdinand of Austria-Este on 28 June 1914. Within weeks of this event the Great Powers had fired off volleys of ultimata to each other. On 28 July Austria-Hungary declared war on Serbia. On 1 August Germany declared war on Russia and followed this up two days later by declaring war on France. Germany had planned meticulously for this eventuality. Fortunately for the Allied forces, the execution of General von Schlieffen's plan, which aimed to avoid waging war on both the western and eastern fronts simultaneously, did not work out as neatly on the ground as it had on paper and the German army was eventually worn down.

THE PEACE 'SETTLEMENT' GIVES RISE TO SMOULDERING RESENTMENT

The catalogue of death and destruction after four years of international war is well documented. The most devastating consequence of the war, as far as European relations were concerned, was that the subsequent peace conference did not attempt to consult the defeated nations. Germany, which was expected to meet the full cost of the war through a series of punitive reparation payments, was as resentful of the peace terms or *diktat* as France had been after the Franco-Prussian war. In his book *The Economic Consequences of Peace* (1919) the economist John Maynard Keynes criticized the reparation payments on the grounds that they would undermine Germany economically and that this was not in the best interests of Europe as a whole.

The most devastating consequence of the war was that the subsequent peace conference did not attempt to consult the defeated nations.

The conference made some attempt to address the myriad of outstanding territorial claims along the lines of the principles outlined in President Wilson's 14-point peace plan (1918).

A free, open-minded and absolutely impartial adjustment of all colonial claims, based upon a strict observance of the principle that in determining all such questions of sovereignty the interests of the populations concerned must have equal weight with the equitable claims of the government whose title is to be determined (Wilson, 1927).

However, this principle proved difficult to implement in practice, particularly in Eastern Europe where there was a confused geographic spread of ethnic and cultural groupings. The map of Europe had undergone a significant change. Alsace-Lorraine, the 'political football' of Franco-German relations, went back to the French. Overall, Europe went from being a continent of 19 monarchies and 3 republics before the war to one of 14 monarchies and 16 republics after it (Davies, 1997). Inevitably such a dramatic redefinition of national boundaries was going to cause some dissatisfaction.

SECOND WORLD WAR

Historians now tend to agree that the First and Second World Wars were not separate events but rather two episodes within the same drama. Although the First World War was dubbed 'the war to end all wars' there was no feeling of finality about the subsequent Paris peace conference. For different reasons, Britain, Russia and America had turned their attention away from continental Europe and France was left feeling very vulnerable. To try and tilt the balance of power in her favour, France's foreign policy after the First World War had two overriding objectives: one was to keep Germany economically weak and the other was to bolster her own security by forging new alliances with the Eastern European countries of Poland, Czechoslovakia, Romania and Yugoslavia.

The tide of events was, however, turning against the French. Germany's wounded national pride coupled with the economic depression found a sympathetic spokesman in the form of Adolf Hitler. Anxious not to repeat the mistakes of 1914, Hitler did not want to have to fight a war on two fronts and he therefore made a non-aggression pact with the Soviet Union. This ensured that after Austria, Czechoslovakia and Poland became the first casualties of Hitler's search for *lebensraum* or 'living space', there was no risk of a Soviet reprisal. In April 1940 Hitler buttressed his northern front by invading Denmark and Norway and in May of the same year he was ready to attack the old arch-enemy, France. German forces overran Holland and Belgium in 18 days. They then marched through northern France and took the Channel ports, thereby cutting off further British assistance. Within weeks German troops had reached Paris. Memories of the events 70 years earlier remained deeply embedded in the French psyche and, rather than risk a repetition of the siege of 1870, they capitulated, declaring Paris an 'open city'. In the armistice signed on 22 June 1940 Marshal Pétain agreed to German military occupancy of northern France, leaving a French government – under strict German supervision – to administer the central and Mediterranean regions from the city of Vichy. Alsace-Lorraine was kicked back to Germany. For four years until the Allied forces landed in France on 6 June 1944, most of Europe remained under the tyranny of Nazi occupation. It was a traumatic experience that was to shape the political mindset of a whole continent.

Chapter 2

....

EUROPE'S SEARCH FOR
A NEW ORDER

After the Second World War, the great clear up operation had to begin. The American Marshall Plan provided enormous financial assistance with the physical reconstruction of the continent. Almost more important, however, was the question of how to stop France and Germany coming to blows again. The European Coal and Steel Community agreement was a breakthrough in establishing better relations between the two countries – not least because it made it physically more difficult for them to construct the weapons of war.

BY 1945 EUROPE HAD LITERALLY FOUGHT ITSELF INTO THE GROUND

In 1945 Europe lay in ruins. The technological advances spawned from the industrial revolution a century earlier had been used to flatten towns and cities with appalling consequences to human life. Millions of refugees were starving and, with the infrastructure of central Europe in disarray, it was an immensely difficult task to repatriate them.

One of the remarkable things about the history of the human race is that at its darkest moments individuals of great courage and vision surface. In 1945, after France had been invaded three times in 70 years, Franco-German relations were at a nadir and it would have been only too easy for the post-war years to become mired in bitter recriminations and mistrust. However, well before 1945 a number of key people realized that, once the war was over, a new order would need to be fashioned that would make war between France and Germany impossible. In the post-war years the French statesman Robert Schuman spearheaded the drive towards the construction of supranational institutions that would override national jealousies.

THE MARSHALL PLAN

In the immediate aftermath of the war Germany was divided into four separate zones, each of which was to come under the military control of either the American, British, French or Soviet forces. Berlin, which was in the middle of the Soviet zone, was also split into four different sectors each of which was administered by one of the four Allies. But European resources were severely limited and trying to sort out the administrative chaos as well as keeping a watchful eye on Soviet machinations in places as far apart as Greece and Persia was stretching them too far.

It became clear to President Truman that America's obligations to Europe could not end with the close of hostilities. Without US financial assistance, it would take the European countries years to rebuild their industrial base and a prolonged recovery period could trigger another global depression. Furthermore, the balance of power in Europe had undergone a seismic shift; an economically strong and cohesive Western Europe was needed to counterbalance the growing threat of Soviet Russia. In June 1947 the US Secretary of State, George Marshall, put forward a radical proposal for the US to finance the reconstruction of Europe. He explained,

> *It became clear that America's obligations to Europe could not end with the close of hostilities.*

'It is logical that the United States should do whatever it is able to do to assist in the return of normal economic health in the world, without which there can be no political stability and no assured peace' (Thomson, 1967). This assistance was to be offered to all parties to the conflict that wanted to avail themselves of it. The only condition was that the recipient nation should put up a sum equal to the funds they received from the US. The Russians were hostile to what they perceived as a ploy to stave off bankruptcy by the capitalist world and not only did they refuse to participate in the aid themselves but they also prevented their Eastern European satellites from doing so.

In order to administer aid from the Marshall Plan, the Organization for European Economic Co-operation (OEEC) was set up and from 1948 to 1951 $12,500m was distributed to 16 countries (Davies, 1997). But each of these countries made unilateral investment decisions and the implementation of the Plan did little to foster a spirit of reconciliation between the recipients. By the late 1940s relations between France and Germany were decidedly fractious. Germany under Chancellor Adenauer chafed at the restrictions over economic and foreign policy while France reacted with hostility to any proposals which threatened to undermine her conviction that the only safe Germany was an economically weak one.

FRANCO-GERMAN RELATIONS BECOME RATHER FRAYED

It was France's fear that restoring Germany's industrial potential would be tantamount to restoring her military might that provoked the most serious post-war rift between the two countries – the control of the coal-mining Saar region. This area had been returned to Germany in 1935 but, in December 1946, it was taken out of the 'zoning agreement' and put under the economic control of the French. The move was approved by the *Landtag*, the locally elected legislative assembly, but it nevertheless provoked outrage in Germany. At the end of a visit to Germany in 1950 by the French foreign minister, Robert Schuman, Chancellor Adenauer told a press conference that the Saar was German in law, language and spirit (Willis, 1969).

THE SCHUMAN PLAN

It was at this low ebb in Franco-German relations that Robert Schuman suddenly announced a radical proposal that was to set the policies of both countries on an entirely new direction: the pooling of the French and German coal and steel industries. The idea was the brain-child of Jean Monnet who at the time was the head of the Commissariat du Plan de Modernisation et d'Équipement, the institution charged with rebuilding France's industrial base. Monnet, an economist by training, had had an extremely varied career, including a spell as the Deputy Secretary-General of the League of Nations and, during the inter-war period, he acted as a roving economic troubleshooter for foreign governments. He had strong links with Britain and America and it was he who really first championed the idea of a United States of Europe.

The plan to amalgamate France and Germany's coal and steel production was prepared in total secrecy. Chancellor Adenauer was told of the idea only on the morning that Robert Schuman delivered his dramatic press conference but he immediately gave it his approval. The original proposal was to include the UK, Italy and the Benelux countries as well as France and Germany. The British government, however, declined to participate, thereby consigning the UK to being a peripheral player in European affairs for the next 20 years.

The European Coal and Steel Community was agreed in 1951 and came into effect the following year. Its stated objectives were the establishment of a single market in these two basic industries and the formation of a uniform code of regulations governing production and competition. But the political sub-agenda was far more important. By pooling the industrial base of Western Europe, it would effectively be impossible for individual countries to indulge in the sort of armament building programmes that had occurred earlier in the twentieth century.

The proponents of an integrated Europe did not have an easy time translating their vision into policies. The Schuman Plan was only ratified after an immense struggle. There remained a huge body of opinion in both France and Germany that was wholly resistant to any sort of rapprochement, let alone integration, and the path towards closer union in the latter part of the twentieth century is really a history of the struggle between these two opposing forces. The establishment of the Coal and Steel Community, however, marked a major turning-point in Franco-German relations.

Chapter 3

THE ROAD TO THE TREATY OF ROME

The coal and steel agreement was not the only area in which the governments of Western Europe co-ordinated policy. The idea of the European movement was to proceed with integration along three broad planks of policy: economic, political and military. Once a viable economic and political framework had been constructed, it was hoped to incorporate what would always be the more contentious and sensitive issue – military policy. However, fate has a habit of throwing a spanner in the works of neatly crafted plans. And in this case it was the Korean war that brought military policy to the top of the agenda. An attempt to construct a European fighting force almost derailed the integration movement but it recovered and went on to forge the Treaty of Rome, which was an enormous milestone along the road to greater European integration.

THE FIRST STEPS TOWARDS POLITICAL CO-ORDINATION

The roots of closer political integration were embedded in the Council of Europe which was set up on 5 May 1949. The ten founding members were Belgium, Denmark, France, Britain, Ireland, Italy, the Netherlands, Luxembourg, Norway and Sweden. A year later Germany was admitted. Its aim was, according to the first article of the statute, 'to achieve greater unity between its members for the purposes of safeguarding and realising the ideals and principles which are their common heritage and facilitating their economic and social progress' (Robertson, 1956).

Right from the start, countries polarized into those that saw the Council as the beginning of a supranational body to which nation states would gradually abrogate part of their sovereignty and those which saw its function as purely consultative. Nevertheless, in the charged atmosphere after the Second World War any organization that fostered closer co-operation between European nations was viewed as a force for good and other countries quickly applied to join its ranks. There are now 34 members of the Council of Europe but, as a vehicle for furthering integration, it did not prove as effective as its creators had had hoped it would be.

THE EUROPEAN COAL AND STEEL COMMUNITY

This role really fell to the European Coal and Steel Community (ECSC). Four institutions were created as a result of the Treaty of Paris on 18 April 1951 to supervise the setting-up and running of the ECSC:

1 A High Authority
2 A Council of Ministers
3 A Common Assembly
4 A Court of Justice

Apart from making war between France and Germany physically more difficult, the ECSC's significance lay in the fact that it established an operating and administrative framework for supranational co-operation – the broad design of which still exists today.

The inclusion of a Court of Justice was also an important step in creating a European entity since it anchored the ECSC firmly into a rule of law outside the jurisdiction of national legal systems

KOREA FORCES THE PACE OVER MILITARY CO-OPERATION

After the traumatic experiences of the previous 75 years, it was not surprising that some form of military co-operation was considered to be a major priority for the new European structure. The territorial decisions agreed between the Big Three – the USA, Russia and the UK – at their conferences at Yalta (February 1945) and Potsdam (July/August 1945) were to pave the way for the gradual drawing across Eastern Europe of what Churchill dubbed the 'iron curtain'. This East–West divide was to play an important part in fostering closer relations between the countries of Western Europe.

In 1948 Britain, France, Belgium, the Netherlands and Luxembourg agreed to take joint defensive action in the event of any renewed German aggression. As well as committing the signatories to a policy of mutual self-defence, the Treaty of Brussels also contained a loose agreement to co-operate on economic, social and cultural matters. A year later, this agreement was extended to include the US, Canada, Italy, Iceland, Norway, Denmark and Portugal and became known as the North Atlantic Treaty Organization (NATO).

The invasion of South Korea on 25 June 1950 threw the question of Europe's defence into sharp focus. As far as the Americans were concerned, it confirmed their suspicions about communism's expansionist tendencies and they consequently pressed for German rearmament in order to have a more effective eastern bulkhead against the threat of Soviet invasion.

FRANCE REJECTS PROPOSALS FOR A EUROPEAN DEFENCE COMMUNITY

In October 1950 the French prime minister, René Pleven, suggested forming an integrated European army that would include German troops. Negotiations about what became known as the Pleven Plan were extremely protracted but eventually a treaty proposing the formation of the European Defence Community (EDC) was signed on 27 May 1952. This restored – as far as was possible without Russian agreement – sovereignty to West Germany and also permitted the formation of some German units as part of a European defence force. French opinion was, however, still sharply divided over the question of German rearmament and when Prime Minister Mendès-France tried to ratify the treaty in the French Assembly on 20 August 1954 it was rejected by a vote of 319–264 (Willis, 1969).

The architects of grand visions always experience setbacks along the road to their goal but for the European integrationists the collapse of the EDC seemed not so much a setback as a black hole. Its failure also snuffed out attempts to form a European Political Community. Nine years after the cessation of hostilities, Europe was therefore left with no plan to re-admit Germany back into its fold. This had gradually come to be widely accepted as the only way of containing 'the German problem'. The theory was that, if Germany became inextricably linked with its neighbours through a series of economic, political and military ties, it would not be in its interest to wage war on them. Clearly, the first step was to grant sovereignty to West Germany but the prospects for doing this had receded and, not surprisingly, within Germany there was enormous resentment towards the French.

> *For the European integrationists the collapse of the EDC seemed not so much a setback as a black hole.*

Frantic efforts were made to come up with some sort of alternative plan. Inspiration came to the British foreign secretary where so many great ideas have been hatched – in his bath (Willis, 1969). Anthony Eden proposed that the Brussels Treaty of 1948 could be reworked to form a new European grouping, the Western Europe Union, which would include both Germany and Italy. There was no organizational structure to back up this body; it was essentially just a committee made up of the foreign ministers of the countries concerned. The Western Europe Union was therefore intergovernmental rather than supranational and its main contribution to European integration was that it provided a vehicle for readmitting Germany into the comity of Western European nations, thus paving the way for closer economic co-operation. The 1955 Paris Accords recognized German sovereignty, admitted Germany and Italy to NATO and made provision for the ending of the Western powers' occupation of the Federal Republic. It was now implicitly acknowledged that Russia – their former ally – posed the greatest threat to the peace of Europe.

TREATY OF ROME

After the struggles over the EDC and the Council of Europe's rather ineffectual attempts at forging closer co-operation, it was becoming increasingly evident that economic policy was going to provide the most effective route to integration. At a meeting of the foreign ministers of the six ECSC members in Messina in Italy on 3 June 1955 this was formally recognized. Their final communiqué read:

> The governments of Belgium, France, the Federal Republic of Germany, Italy, Luxembourg and the Netherlands consider that the moment has arrived to initiate a new phase on the path of constructing Europe. They believe that this has to be done principally in the economic sphere, and regard it as necessary to continue the creation of a United Europe through the expansion of joint institutions, the gradual fusion of

national economies, the creation of a common market and the gradual co-ordination of social policies (Cox, 1992).

An intergovernmental committee was immediately set up under the chairmanship of Paul-Henri Spaak, an ardent federalist. It reported back to the ECSC Assembly on March 1956 with two main proposals. These were the setting-up of a common market – which would be known as the European Economic Community (EEC) – and the creation of a European Atomic Energy Community (Euratom). Both of these proposals were essentially encapsulated in the Treaties of Rome on 25 May 1957.

The provisions of the treaty pertaining to the common market were far-reaching and included the phased abolition of trade tariffs and quotas over a 12-year period, the adoption of common policies on agriculture and transport and the free movement of labour and capital. The treaty also paved the way for the setting-up of the European Investment Bank and the European Social Fund.

The institutional framework for administering the common market was broadly similar to that established for the ECSC, namely:

1 A Commission
2 A Council
3 An Assembly
4 A Court of Justice

The Commission's role was to initiate proposals and to look at questions from a broad European perspective while the interests of individual countries were represented by the Council of Ministers, which was the executive arm of the structure. Since 1979, members of the Parliamentary Assembly have been directly elected by the electorate of the member countries. The purpose of the Assembly was to inject a democratic element into the supranational system – albeit only in an advisory capacity.

A second treaty was also signed on 25 May 1957, which set up the European Atomic Energy Community (Euratom). Apart from the practical difficulties of setting up a nuclear capability in each of the EEC countries, nuclear energy was a natural contender for Europeanization as it was a new industry and therefore there were no well-entrenched national vested interests.

Chapter 4

....

DEVELOPMENT OF THE EUROPEAN MONETARY SYSTEM

The 1960s were a difficult decade for the European Community. Some progress was made in whittling down trade tariffs and the implementation of the Common Agricultural Policy in 1968 was a significant milestone since, for many years, it was the only area in which the community could claim to operate a truly common policy. But for much of the decade France and Germany were at loggerheads over the future shape and structure of the EEC. In the 1970s agreement was finally reached over enlarging the Community. Britain, Denmark and Ireland joined the inner core of Six but enlargement brought its own problems. For much of the 1970s the heads of government were so busy trying to steer their own economies through a series of financial and economic squalls that European integration took second place. However, partly in response to the unsettled international background, the Community did in the 1970s take the first faltering steps towards economic and monetary union.

DE GAULLE STANDS FIRM AGAINST ENLARGEMENT

General de Gaulle's *idée fixe* about France's rightful place in the world order powerfully shaped inter-European relations during the 1960s. In 1963 he summarized these ambitions succinctly: 'To be prosperous, our own master and powerful' (Willis, 1969).

The first issue that divided France from its five partners was the question of whether the EEC should be expanded to include other countries. Israel was the first country to apply for membership in 1958, followed shortly afterwards by Greece and Turkey. But it was really Britain that the EEC members – apart from France – were hoping would join their ranks. The smaller countries felt that Britain would provide a useful counterbalance to the Franco-German axis while Germany was attracted by the trading opportunities that UK membership would bring.

Prior to the formation of the EEC, a plan had been mooted by the British to establish a Europe-wide free trade area. However, once six countries had opted to form their own economic community, the remaining seven – Austria, Denmark, Norway, Portugal, Sweden, Switzerland and the UK – pressed on with the establishment of the European Free Trade Area (EFTA) in 1959. Just 18 months later the Macmillan government had a change of heart and decided that it would be both politically and economically more expedient to join the EEC and an application was therefore submitted on 10 August 1961. The negotiations were protracted but towards the end of 1962 it seemed as if the various parties were finally close to reaching an agreement when, completely out of the blue, at a press conference in January 1963 de Gaulle dropped the bombshell that he would veto the UK's application. His reasons were that Britain's focus was still predominantly towards the US and the Commonwealth and it was not sufficiently European in its outlook to fit harmoniously in with the rest of the community. As Common Market decisions required unanimity this was the end of the matter.

> *In January 1963 de Gaulle dropped the bombshell that he would veto the UK's application.*

The question of whether to press ahead with geographical enlargement before complete integration has been achieved by a small inner core has always been a difficult one for the European movement. But, in blocking the UK's membership of the EEC, de Gaulle lost a potential ally over the fundamental issue of what type of structure the EEC should assume. His view of Europe as an association of nations that should collaborate over a range of issues was much closer to the British view than that of the other five EEC members who all saw the formation of a supranational entity as their ultimate goal. And it was this difference in perception that was to block progress towards closer integration for the rest of the decade.

The Germans were particularly annoyed at what was seen as de Gaulle's high-handed action in blocking Britain's membership but Chancellor Adenauer believed that, for the good of Europe as a whole, relations between his country and France were of paramount importance, and so only days later on 22 January 1963 he signed a Franco-German treaty of co-operation. This pledged the two countries to consult each other on 'all important questions of foreign policy with a view to reaching, in so far as possible, a similar position' (Willis, 1969). There were also to be six-monthly meetings between the two heads of state and an organization was set up to foster closer relations between the youth of both countries. The treaty marked the high point of Franco-German relations for many years to come.

FRANCO-GERMAN RELATIONS BECOME STRAINED

Later in 1963 Adenauer was forced to step down and he was replaced by Ludwig Erhard who did not attach the same priority to Franco-German relations as his predecessor. Erhard saw Europe developing within an Atlantic alliance. Relations between the two countries became extremely strained in 1965 when, for a period of seven months, the French operated an 'empty chair' policy at the Council of Ministers meetings thereby blocking discussion of any substantive matters. At issue was a package of proposals that included a move towards a system of majority voting. This stalemate was eventually resolved at the Luxembourg summit in January 1966 by a decision not to impose majority voting on issues where one member had a particular interest. Thus the veto was effectively retained as a result of the 'Luxembourg Compromise'. And in 1967 de Gaulle once again exercised his right to use it: he vetoed Britain's second attempt to join the EEC.

The other major area of contention between de Gaulle and the other five members of the EEC was defence policy. De Gaulle was extremely suspicious of America's influence in Europe. After the ignominy of the last war and subsequent problems with its colonies, he believed it was essential that France should regain military independence rather than rely on the Americans. The French therefore developed their own nuclear deterrent and gradually withdrew from NATO.

De Gaulle finally retired in 1969 and one of the first acts of his successor, Georges Pompidou, was to call a meeting of the EEC heads of government in order to try and recast the European debate. At the Hague summit in December 1969 a number of important decisions were made. It was agreed that the community should be enlarged. The goal of political and monetary union was confirmed and, to this end, two committees were set up. The first, chaired by Pierre Werner (the then prime minister of Luxembourg), was to look into implementing monetary union and the second, chaired by Étienne Davignon (a Belgian diplomat and later an EC Commissioner), would make recommendations on political union. A number of other specific funding decisions were taken and the European Parliament's budgetary powers were broadened.

ENLARGEMENT

In 1973 Britain, together with Denmark and Ireland, finally joined the European club. (Norway applied at the same time and signed the treaty of accession. But when the treaty was put to a national referendum, it was defeated.) Political democracy was a prerequisite for full membership of the Community and thus Greece, Spain and Portugal were effectively barred for a number of years. However, once they had overthrown their military regimes, their applications were considered. Greece became a member on 1 January 1981 while Spain and Portugal were admitted five years later. The Community of 12 was expanded again in 1995 when Austria, Finland and Sweden joined.

FIRST ATTEMPT TO CO-ORDINATE
MONETARY POLICY

Once agreement had been reached over the establishment of a customs union, it was a natural progression to look at ways of harmonizing monetary and economic policies. The 1970 Werner report had recommended the integration of Europe's capital markets, setting up a European central bank and irrevocably fixing exchange rate parities, preferably prior to establishing a common currency. All of which, the report suggested, should be achieveable within a period of ten years.

The collapse of the Bretton Woods system of fixed exchange rates in 1971 gave an added spur to these monetary deliberations. In an attempt to try and dampen exchange rate fluctuations between European currencies a 'snake' was introduced which permitted rates to move within a 4.5 per cent range (i.e. ± 2.25 per cent). But it was not a particularly fortuitous time to undertake an exercise in currency management. The following year was an extremely turbulent one. The dollar depreciated sharply after it was allowed to

The collapse of the Bretton Woods system of fixed exchange rates in 1971 gave an added spur to monetary deliberations.

float in March 1973. The Yom Kippur war broke out in October and OPEC discovered the economic power of a cartel with the result that, by December, oil prices had quadrupled. The resulting economic downturn caused immense problems for the European economies. In the light of these developments, it is perhaps not surprising that the 'snake' was not very successful at maintaining exchange rate stability.

THE EUROPEAN MONETARY SYSTEM

Towards the end of the 1970s it was apparent that, if the European currencies were to achieve any degree of stability, the 'snake' needed a radical overhaul. Roy Jenkins, the president of the Commission from 1977 to 1981, is largely credited with launching its more wide-ranging successor, the European Monetary System (EMS). Importantly, the scheme was also given the enthusiastic backing of both the French president, Valéry Giscard d'Estaing, and the German Chancellor, Helmut Schmidt.

The EMS was launched on 13 March 1979 and involved eight of the nine EEC member countries with the UK, as usual, opting to watch from the sidelines. A new common unit of account, the European Currency Unit or ECU, was introduced which was a cocktail of all the EEC currencies (including sterling) mixed in proportion to each country's relative economic size. The idea of using a common unit of account dated back to the 1950s when the six original EEC members formed a European Payments Union and used a European unit of account (EUA) equivalent to the same fixed amount of gold as one US dollar to calculate intergovernment transactions.

Under the EMS, an exchange mechanism (ERM) was set up that permitted currencies to fluctuate 2.25 per cent on either side of their central ECU rate. Italy was initially allowed a wider 6 per cent band (which also applied to Spain and the UK when they joined the system in 1989 and 1990 respectively). When the cross rate of two currencies strayed outside the permitted bands, there was an obligation on both of the central banks concerned to intervene to bring the rate back inside the system. In practice, however, the onus tended to fall on the weaker currency and a credit system provided financial support to governments whose currencies fell foul of market pressures.

The EMS came under repeated speculative attacks, forcing realignments of the currency parameters. The markets were, however, only reflecting the fact that the attempt to forge a closer monetary union was not being backed by any economic convergence. This point was forcefully impressed on Jacques Delors who, as France's finance minister from 1981 to 1984, had the thankless task of trying to protect the franc from some tremendous batterings on the foreign exchange market.

Ironically, although monetary and economic policy was eventually to forge the path towards closer union, the initial moves in this direction were taken in response to external events rather than as part of any grand design to promote greater integration.

BUDGETARY PRESSURES

Apart from an array of international problems, the EEC also had to deal with its own budgetary crisis in the 1970s. The growing latticework of policies and committees needed funding and the costs of the common agricultural policy had escalated dramatically. Britain was one of the major net contributors to the EEC budget and the Prime Minister Mrs Thatcher insisted that sorting out the budgetary problems was the community's top priority.

Chapter 5

FRESH IMPETUS TOWARDS ECONOMIC AND MONETARY UNION

The EEC entered the 1980s in a mood of great despondency. Individual economies were plunging into recession and most of the community's time seemed to be taken up with bickering over money. The Treaty of Rome's timetable for the elimination of all trade barriers by 1970 had been blown hopelessly off course. The European idealism that had so fired the early years of the community had completely evaporated. The collapse of communism, however, at the end of the decade gave a completely new twist to the European kaleidoscope and, indirectly, provided a fresh impetus to EMU.

GRASPING THE BUDGETARY NETTLE

In May 1981, François Mitterrand had at last realized his ambition of becoming President of France and, like so many of his predecessors, felt it was his duty to reassert France's primacy in European affairs. His first opportunity to play a decisive role came when France held the presidency of the Council in 1984. The rows about Britain's contribution to the EEC budget had been building up steadily in the early 1980s and, at the Fontainbleau summit meeting in June 1984, Mitterrand decided to grasp the budgetary nettle. A solution was eventually arrived at which, if it did not fully satisfy

33

Mrs Thatcher, at least placated her sufficiently to allow discussion of other issues. One of these was the directionless drift that the community had slipped into. It was therefore decided that James Dooge (a former Irish foreign minister) should head up a committee to look at the best way of refocusing the Community's efforts. The committee produced a raft of proposals designed to reactivate the phased withdrawal of all impediments to cross-border trade in Europe. This became the blueprint for the 1992 Single European Act.

THE SINGLE EUROPEAN ACT

Agreement to the Single European Act was finally hammered out at the Luxembourg summit in December 1985. It had far more wide-ranging implications for European integration than its rather simple title suggests. Apart from identifying almost 300 impediments to the free movement of goods, people, services and capital, it also included an extension to the system of qualified majority voting in the Council of Ministers and a commitment to monetary and economic union. The story of Europe's integration is littered with allusions to trains but a spacecraft is probably a more apt metaphor. At various critical stages, a new rocket has been fired that takes the vehicle into a new orbit. The Single European Act was the rocket that, to borrow Delors's own phrase, would launch 'a Europe without frontiers'.

THE DELORS REPORT

With the concept of a common market now back on track, it was time to turn again to the question of economic and monetary union. At the Hanover summit in June 1988, the president of the European Commission, Jacques Delors, was appointed the chairman of a committee charged with not only looking at economic and monetary union in general terms but also suggesting a series of stages by which it could be implemented. The committee was made up of the 12 governors of the European central banks, a commissioner and three independent advisors. It came to the conclusion that economic and monetary union should be a three-staged process:

- *Stage One*: Greater emphasis on co-ordinating national economic and monetary policies.
- *Stage Two*: The Community would lay down a set of budgetary and economic guidelines and individual governments should tailor their domestic policies in such a way as to ensure that they meet these. A European System of Central Banks (ESCB) to be set up to take over all EC monetary functions and to co-ordinate national monetary policies.
- *Stage Three:* Lock the exchange rates of the participating countries irrevocably together with a view to creating a single currency.

The committee delivered its recommendations in April 1989 and, at the Strasbourg summit the following December, it was decided to hold an intergovernmental conference (IGC) to discuss the changes that would have to be made to the Treaty of Rome in order to implement this phased monetary and economic union. At the Dublin summit in April 1990 agreement was reached to set up a second parallel intergovernmental conference to consider political union. The findings of the two IGCs would be considered at the Maastricht summit in 1991.

THE COLLAPSE OF COMMUNISM

While Western Europe was busy trying to come to terms with the idea of these economic and monetary proposals, a dramatic subplot was unfolding in the eastern part of the continent that was to have major implications for Europe as a whole. With the collapse of communism and the unification of the two Germanys, the question of German nationalism again reared its head. For different reasons (which are discussed later), both Germany and France felt that the best way of addressing these fears would be to knit Germany more tightly into a union with Europe. The disintegration of the Soviet Union therefore injected a new urgency into the process of economic and monetary union.

> *A dramatic sub-plot was unfolding in the eastern part of the continent that was to have major implications for Europe as a whole.*

MAASTRICHT TREATY

The Treaty of European Union was the centrepiece of the Maastricht summit in December 1991. Article A described the treaty as marking 'a new stage in the process of creating an ever closer union among the peoples of Europe'. In practice, it fired the next rocket that would take the community a long way forward along the trajectory towards an integrated union. The main body of the treaty laid down the steps by which economic and monetary union would be achieved but the treaty also included a Social Chapter and established the principle that eventually common foreign and defence policies would be adopted.

John Major, who had taken over as Prime Minister from Mrs Thatcher, negotiated an opt-out clause on both the Social Chapter and EMU for the UK. At Britain's insistence all references to the politically charged phrase 'federalism' were removed and the concept of 'subsidiarity' was introduced whereby as many decisions as possible would devolve down to the national level, as opposed to being taken at the supranational level in Brussels.

The main points of the chapters covering economic and monetary union were that member states were required to pursue national policies that would result in their economies meeting the guidelines laid down by the Council. It was stipulated that countries should not run excessive debts but, in any event, the community would not be responsible for the debt of any member country.

In order to co-ordinate and monitor monetary policy, the individual central banks would form the European System of Central Banks whose primary objective was to maintain price stability. At the beginning of Stage Two, a European Monetary Institute (EMI) would be set up to oversee the move to a single currency and the establishment of a European Central Bank (ECB). At the end of Stage Two, the heads of government would meet to decide which countries qualified to move onto Stage Three. At this point, their currencies would be irrevocably locked together and they would eventually be merged into a single currency, the euro. In order to become eligible to embark on Stage Three, countries had to meet the following criteria:

- countries should have a budget deficit of 3 per cent or less of GDP
- the ratio of gross national debt to GDP should not exceed 60 per cent of GDP
- inflation should not exceed by more than 1.5 per cent the average of the three best performers
- member countries must maintain their exchange rates within the permitted bands of the exchange rate mechanism for at least two years
- long-term interest rates must not deviate more than 2 per cent from the the interest rates of the three lowest inflation countries.

THE ELECTORATES' RESERVATIONS

The treaty was finally signed in February 1992. At the time few, if any, people had any idea how difficult it would be to achieve the necessary ratification in the member countries. The Danes delivered the first shock when they voted in a referendum by 50.7 per cent against the treaty. Desperate not to be left out of the European club, the Danish government decided the treaty would be more acceptable to their electorate if they incorporated some opt-out clauses, rather as the British had done. Although the foreign ministers had ruled out making any alterations to the Maastricht treaty, Denmark was allowed to opt out of EMU as well as any future defence policies and the enforcement of European citizenship. On the basis of these 'amendments' (as opposed to outright changes) the treaty was again put to a referendum in May 1993 and this time managed to produce a 'yes' majority of 56.7 per cent.

France held a referendum in September 1992 which, to Mitterrand's chagrin, only produced a 'yes' vote by the slimmest of margins. Probably the hardest battle was fought in the UK where the prime minister had to overcome a very strong rear-guard action from within his own Conservative party but ratification was achieved in July 1993. Germany was the last country to ratify the treaty. And even here there was a sting in the tail. The Bundestag ratified the treaty but only on condition that there was a later vote on its actual implementation. The difficulties in achieving ratification of the treaty demonstrated the problem that the integrationist movement has had in carrying the people of Europe with it.

THE MARKETS' RESERVATIONS

The financial markets were also very uncertain about the whole idea of monetary union. In September 1992 at the height of the struggle to secure ratification of the treaty, the foreign exchange markets launched a speculative attack against the pound and the lira, forcing both to leave the exchange rate mechanism. By the end of the year Spain and Portugal had also been forced to devalue. But the market had not finished and in the summer pressure began to build up on the French

> *At the height of the struggle to secure ratification of the treaty, the foreign exchange markets launched a speculative attack against the pound and the lira.*

franc. After a series of crisis meetings, it was decided to widen the permitted bands of fluctuation to 15 per cent on either side of a currency's central rate.

ELEVEN COUNTRIES DECLARED EMU-READY

In the mid-1990s the prospects of any country, apart from Luxembourg, achieving the Maastricht criteria looked poor. Even Germany was struggling to meet the criterion that its public sector deficit should not exceed 3 per cent of GDP. But thanks to a turnaround in the economic cycle and some creative accounting, the intergovernmental conference in May 1998 was able to declare that 11 of the 12 applicant countries were eligible to move on to Stage Three of EMU on 1 January 1999. Only Greece was judged not to have met the necessary criteria but it was hoped that it might become eligible in 2001. The UK, Denmark and Sweden opted not to join the first wave.

Stage Three of EMU will be a transitional period during which member states gradually switch from their national currencies to the euro. From 1 January 1999 the European central bank has taken over monetary policy from the national central banks. New public debt is being issued in euros. On 1 January 2002, euro currency notes and coins will go into circulation and national notes and coinage will gradually be phased out.

Chapter 6

POLITICAL FACTORS RESURFACE

Running all the way through the history of European integration there has been a strong political undercurrent. In the years immediately after the Second World War it was seen as absolutely essential for the long-term peace of Europe that a solution was found to the 'German problem'. It quickly became apparent that the French idea of keeping Germany economically weak was not a realistic proposition and that incorporating the German people into an integrated Europe was the best way of preventing a resurgence of any overly nationalistic tendencies.

In the early years of the Community, the goal was quite explicitly political union and each phase of the integration process was seen as just another step towards this ultimate objective. Paul-Henri Spaak, addressing the Council of Europe in 1964, explained that the architects of the Treaty of Rome 'did not think of it as essentially economic; they thought of it as a stage on the way to political union' (Urwin, 1991). And Chancellor Adenauer pressed the idea of the Common Market on his reluctant economics minister, Ludwig Erhard, on the grounds that it was a means of achieving political integration. After the formation of the Common Market in 1958, however, there then followed a period of 30 years when the political element of integration was relegated to a background issue. But it was dramatically catapulted back to the foreground in 1989 with the collapse of the Berlin Wall.

GERMAN RE-UNIFICATION REVIVES OLD QUESTIONS

In the era of the Cold War the Soviet Union seemed the greatest menace to the peace of Europe and the notion of Germany posing a physical threat waned. As a result, the goal of political union lost its sense of urgency. However, in 1989 the re-unification of Germany reawakened the old fears about a strong Germany in the heart of Europe. This was to prove to be another defining moment in the path to integration since it prompted President Mitterrand and Chancellor Kohl to put their combined efforts into turning the ERM from being just a mechanical system designed to smooth the wheels of commerce within Europe into a vehicle for achieving a far greater degree of political unity.

The determination of the French and German leaders to inject a fresh impetus into economic and monetary union was critical. Had it not been for this renewed commitment from the Franco-German axis, EMU may well have floundered in the face of so many obstacles in the early 1990s.

Mitterrand's reasons for wanting to press ahead rapidly with the policy of integration were relatively straightforward. He was concerned that an enlarged Germany might not feel such a strong need to be part of the European community and, once it slipped outside this structure, it would be far more difficult for France to exert any influence over German policy.

GERMANY'S STRUGGLE TO FIND AN INTERNATIONAL ROLE

The German Chancellor's enthusiasm for political union was more complex. There was certainly a personal element involved. Helmut Kohl wanted to go down as the great unifying Chancellor. He had already secured a place in the history books as the Chancellor who had masterminded the re-unification of the two Germanys and, to add to this, the unification of Europe would overshadow even Bismarck's achievements.

But to see Germany's support of political integration purely in terms of one man's personal crusade is to overlook the colossal difficulty that the German nation has experienced in coming to terms with its past. This collective angst has made it extremely difficult for Germans to find an international role with which they are comfortable and, as a result, Germany punches well below its body weight in the global arena. For example, it does not have a seat on the UN Security Council. Some Germans take the view that it is time to come out of the political wilderness while others, still mindful of the past, feel that it is better to maintain a low profile.

The issue of international joint military operations has highlighted this dichotomy. Germany did not join other NATO countries in sending troops to the Gulf in 1991 on the grounds that the German constitution forbids the deployment of German troops outside NATO countries. But in the international forum this was widely interpreted as Germany shirking its political responsibility. Uncomfortable with this view, Kohl decided to let German forces take part in the United Nations expedition to Somalia in 1993. The SPD party objected strongly and took the matter to the German constitutional court, which ruled that German troops could take part in operations outside the NATO area provided the decision was ratified by parliament.

Europe seems to offer a way out of this political dilemma. Making Germany part of an integrated European union would provide a bridge out of political isolation back onto the world stage. Germans do not have a particularly well-defined national pride; they tend to feel a sense of loyalty to their region and local traditions. Losing a degree of sovereignty and assuming a European identity is not therefore the problem that it is for some other countries –

particularly if it mirrored Germany's own political structure and the union were to take the form of a federation.

Placing Germany within a European context therefore came to have increasing attractions after re-unification and Chancellor Kohl tried to tie in political union as a *quid pro quo* for economic and monetary union. This strategy, however, did not carry the weight of public opinion with it: swapping a German identity for a European one was one thing but swapping the Deutschmark for the euro was quite another. Concern about the loss of the Deutschmark and the financial uncertainties that come with it was an important contributing factor to Helmut Kohl's electoral downfall in September 1998, when he became the first Chancellor in Germany's post-war history to be ousted from power at a general election. The biggest swing against the CDU coalition was in the eastern *Länder* where voters were still suffering the social consequences of the badly managed monetary union.

The demise of Chancellor Kohl marked a generational change and, as such, represented a significant shift in the political landscape of Europe. The triumvirate of Kohl, Mitterrand and Delors was passionately committed to political union as a result of their wartime experiences. In pursuit of their ultimate goal, the political imperative tended to override other considerations. To the next generation of leaders the Second World War is history and, albeit a very significant event, it was not a personally formative experience that has shaped their political credo. As a result, although they are committed to EMU, they are likely to evaluate policies on their inherent merits rather than on whether they contribute to Franco-German reconciliation.

Part

2

HISTORICAL PERSPECTIVE

We should now look at EMU in the context of the history of international monetary relations. Attempts have been made to link currencies together, or to form monetary unions, at regular intervals over the last 150 years, sometimes successfully, sometimes not. These experiences vary from monetary union resulting from political union, as in the examples of Germany and Italy, to currency sharing by independent countries. In this part we will look at these events (in roughly chronological order) and see if any pattern emerges that might have implications for the success of EMU.

Chapter 7

···

HISTORICAL PERSPECTIVE

ITALIAN MONETARY UNION

Before the middle of the nineteenth century, Italy was a collection of a dozen or so separate national states with their own currencies, extending from Piedmont in the north to the Kingdom of the Two Sicilies in the south. The desire emerged in these countries to throw off the long-standing economic and political dominance of their large neighbour Austria. The formation of Italy was secured, surprisingly swiftly, during the 1859–60 period, mainly by the efforts of Cavour, the Prime Minister of Piedmont, who won a military victory over Austria with the help of France. Although more small states were added later, unification was largely complete by 1861. In 1862 the monetary system was also unified across the new country, with the lira introduced as the unit of account throughout the area.

It should be recognized that the working of the monetary system in the nineteenth century was very different from that of today. It was essentially a coinage system, based on the precious metals gold and silver. Some countries based their systems on gold, some on silver, and others, most importantly France, incorporated both. The use of banknotes was becoming increasingly significant, but note issue was not as today solely the prerogative of the central monetary authority, and could also be implemented by private banks. Clearly, this not only prevented any effective control of the

The monetary system in the nineteenth century was essentially a coinage system.

money supply but also led to undue complexity in the domestic monetary system. In times of overissue of banknotes, frequently to finance wars, inflation would ensue and the convertibility of banknotes into the precious-metal coins would inevitably be suspended for long periods.

Such problems of monetary inflation and banking chaos plagued Italy after unification. The new country was economically disorganized and political unity was not popular in the south. Initially, there were no moves to establish a central bank, as a result of resistance from regional interests, and the main commercial banks in the former states continued to issue their own notes. In 1893 the Bank of Italy was finally created out of three of these banks and some semblance of control was established. Real monetary unification was not finalized until 1926, when the Bank of Italy was given monopoly over note issuance and began to operate an effective monetary policy.

The failure to centralize monetary control for a considerable length of time after political union promoted financial instability and severe economic dislocation, which to some extent continues to this day.

GERMAN UNIFICATION

The political unification of Germany entailed a similar sequence of events to that of Italy, but financial and economic developments followed a very different course. In the early nineteenth century Germany consisted of a multitude of different states, all issuing their own coins. However, unlike Italian political unification, the process in Germany was preceded by moves towards economic convergence.

In 1834 the German states founded a customs union, the *Zoll-*

verein, which created a free trade zone throughout the area. Since the multiplicity of coinage systems was seen as an impediment to trade, the monetary system was simplified in 1837. Each state joined one of two currency areas – the northern states adopted the thaler, which was the coinage system of the largest state, Prussia, and the southern states adopted the gulden. Both were based on silver.

Between 1864 and 1871 political unification of the German states was secured as a result of successful wars against Denmark, Austria and France, under the leadership of the Prussian Chancellor Bismarck. Upon the creation of Germany in 1871 the mark was introduced as the new national currency, based on gold.

Unlike the case of Italy, an effective state central bank was quickly created, with the establishment of the Reichsbank in 1875. At this time some 30 commercial banks with the facility to issue notes were in existence, but the Reichsbank immediately took measures to severely curtail this activity. Accordingly, a strong central measure of control was established early on, and the number of note issuing banks declined rapidly. Financial stability henceforth prevailed in Germany for many years until the dislocations caused by the aftermath of the First World War.

The contrast with Italy is illuminating. In Germany economic integration between the states occurred first, and was followed by the stabilization of exchange rates. Political unification came afterwards and monetary union was quickly centralized. In Italy, by contrast, there was no economic integration preceding political unification. Political unification took place somewhat unexpectedly and monetary unification took place much later. Economic integration was left to follow in the wake of these events.

Political union alone does not guarantee a successful monetary union.

The German unification in the nineteenth century would seem

to offer a reassuring precedent for EMU, with a customs union paving the way for a successful monetary unification. But the crucial difference is that the German experience was accompanied by simultaneous political union. The example of Italy, however, shows that political union alone does not guarantee a successful monetary union.

THE CREATION OF THE US FEDERAL RESERVE SYSTEM

The US is a long-standing and effective monetary union. It operates a single monetary policy across a large area, equivalent in size to the area covered by the new European System of Central Banks. However, the structure of US monetary policy as it now exists is actually a relatively recent phenomenon.

The American Civil War (1861–5) created the US as the country we know it today by establishing the dominance of the Federal government over the state governments. National Banking Acts in the 1863–5 period attempted to standardize the country's banking laws, which before the Civil War had varied from state to state. They also sought to limit the freedom of state banks to issue their own notes in favour of nationally chartered banks, but the banking system none the less continued to be highly decentralized. Although the US was a single currency area, no central bank actually existed, and this remained the case into the early 1900s. By this time most other industrialized countries (even Italy) had one. The nature of the banking system proved too inflexible to provide the needs of a rapidly expanding economy. There were periodic money shortages, financial panics and runs on banks. There were also seasonal strains on the system.

After a major banking crisis in 1907 it was decided that a central bank was essential to provide a more 'elastic' supply of money and credit. Because of the continuing strength of regional interests only a loose federal set-up was deemed politically acceptable, as opposed to the highly centralized systems in Germany or the UK. As created in 1913, the US central bank, the Federal Reserve System, divided the country into 12 areas, each with its own Reserve Bank. Each was free to issue its banknotes and to set its own interest rates.

The Federal Reserve's policy at this time was very much geared to stabilizing interest rates, providing enough liquidity to fulfil the requirements of the private sector, and smoothing over seasonal demands for money. Thus it was quite different from the modern implementation of counter-cyclical monetary policy operations.

However, the structure of the Federal Reserve as it then stood created a good deal of confusion, and a power struggle ensued between the the Board of Governors running the system from Washington and the individual Reserve Banks spread throughout the country. From 1922 onwards a gradual centralization of authority began. This gathered pace after the 1929 crash and attendant banking crises, during which it was argued that the Federal Reserve's equivocal structure hampered an efficient response in dealing with the situation. The depth of the crisis enabled the Board in Washington at last to overcome the interests of regional bankers.

With the 1933 Banking Act, the Federal Open Market Committee (FOMC) was created to carry out countrywide monetary policy. This finally centralized the implementation of operations and Reserve Bank interest rates throughout the whole country. The power at the centre was consolidated in 1935, when the number of Reserve Bank Presidents on the FOMC was reduced from twelve to five (each serving on a revolving basis), thus numbering less than the seven members of the Board of Governors. This was a structure that subsequently operated extremely successfully and remains in place to this day.

In this case, we have a situation of political unification having been long established before final monetary unification, in the form of a centralized monetary policy, occurred. This story is similar to that of Italy, with again the erosion of regional monetary authority being an extended and painful process, although the US economy of course was considerably more successful due to its extraordinary resources and flexibility.

The message of this for EMU is that it was right to pass complete power for the implementation of monetary policy immediately to the new European System of Central Banks. But the make-up of the ESCB's governing council is highly decentralized. It comprises six members of the executive board and the eleven governors of the participating central banks. This is in direct contrast to the balance of power in the Federal Reserve, which has operated so effectively since the 1930s.

THE LATIN MONETARY UNION

So far we have looked at monetary unions in which accompanying political unification guaranteed their continuity. Other attempts at union have not been so long lasting. One that is often cited as a bad omen for EMU is the Latin Monetary Union (LMU) established in the mid-nineteenth century.

As noted earlier, France at this time operated a system incorporating both gold and silver coins. France was the dominant economy of Europe and Belgium had linked its currency to the French system in 1832. In addition both Switzerland, upon political unification in 1848, and Italy, in 1861, linked their currencies to that of France, who was their major trading partner. Greece later joined the system. This was formalized in 1865 into the Latin Monetary Union, which stipulated a fixed exchange rate between the member countries and the free circulation of each other's gold and silver coins throughout the area. No provisions were announced for paper money, which remained under the jurisdiction of the individual states.

Problems immediately arose with the practice of gold and silver coins circulating side by side, particularly when the market price of silver fell sharply in the 1870s, so the system effectively moved entirely on to gold.

However, the Union suffered from, firstly, the lack of measures regarding paper money and, secondly, the absence of convergence of national economic policies. The need to finance government spending, especially in Italy, led to the issue of inconvertible paper money, which undermined the maintenance of stable exchange rates.

Because it was a system linking coinage only, the LMU was able to struggle on in some degree until its effective termination at the start of the First World War when all countries ceased fixing their coins to gold.

Clearly this was an extremely limited form of monetary union. Countries' central banks remained fully independent of each other, and there was no attempt to co-ordinate economic policy. The experience was very much reflective of the problems of the time, namely those of basing a monetary system on precious metals, and accommodating the growing requirement for a system incorporating banknotes, rather than coinage alone. What we can conclude from it is that any attempt to form monetary union without political union is a much more problematical affair.

SCANDINAVIAN MONETARY UNION.

Events in Scandinavia saw the formation of a slightly more advanced type of monetary union. It was initially formed in 1872 between Sweden and Denmark, with Norway joining in 1875. At first the system involved the fixing of exchange rates and the adoption of a common coin, the Scandinavian crown (based on gold), to be used throughout the area. But it subsequently went further than the Latin Monetary Union by incorporating in 1885 each country's banknotes, which henceforth circulated freely in the whole area.

The union functioned smoothly for a while, aided by the fact that the three economies were similar in nature, and were linked culturally and linguistically. However, each country retained its own individual central bank, and gradually monetary policies began to diverge. The system effectively ended with the start of the First World War, when all three suspended the convertibility of their banknotes, and the currencies began to drift apart, with the Swedish krona appreciating substantially against the other two due to rising inflation in Norway and Denmark. Attempts to restore the union after the First World War met with limited success, although it was not formally abandoned until 1931.

> *Monetary union is possible for an extended period even with separate central banks, but only so long as underlying economic conditions remain benign.*

This episode demonstrates that monetary union is possible for an extended period even with separate central banks, but only so long as underlying economic conditions remain benign. In addition, proximity and cultural similarity, which assisted the flow of labour, were considerable advantages. But again this fell short of full monetary union and without policy co-ordination and/or political union it was doomed to fail.

OTHER NINETEENTH-CENTURY MONETARY UNIONS

Other attempts to link currencies included the short-lived German/Austrian Monetary Union, which was formed in 1857 and established the use of Prussian silver coinage throughout the area.

This broke down quickly and formally ended when the two went to war in 1867.

Austria and Hungary in 1867 formed a monetary union incorporating a form of political union. The two states remained as separate entities with their own administrations and domestic fiscal policies. But they were both ruled by the same monarch and operated common defence and foreign policies. They shared the same currency, monetary policy and free trade area. This union remained in force until the political union broke up in 1918 and is an interesting example of political union sustaining a monetary union of unlikely partners.

Mention should also be made of the classic period of the gold standard, which held sway briefly from the 1890s to 1914. By the 1890s the major industrialized countries had all moved their monetary systems on to gold. Under the gold standard as it operated at this time, each country's supply of money and credit would in principle rise or fall according to the inflow and outflow of gold as determined by their balance of payments, thereby maintaining stable exchange rates. The system was essentially run by the UK, which had become the dominant industrial and financial power. Since this was a period of general economic stability and prosperity the system functioned smoothly, but was effectively destroyed by the economic upheaval caused by the First World War. This was, however, a system to stabilize exchange rates only, with no accompanying moves to co-ordinate policies or move towards any form of monetary unification.

BELGIUM–LUXEMBOURG ECONOMIC UNION

Although normally regarded as part of Belgium, Luxembourg is actually a separate country. But for many years it formed an economic and monetary union with Belgium. This began as a customs union in 1922 and was formalized into a full monetary union in 1935. It was in fact the only attempt at monetary integration in Europe during the turbulent inter-war period. The two currencies have moved together ever since, until both became absorbed into the euro. Under the union, Belgian and Luxembourg francs were fully interchangeable, although Luxembourg francs were legal tender only in Luxembourg.

GDP in Luxembourg is only 14 billion euros, which makes it one-fifteenth the size of Belgium. Luxembourg has always run its own fiscal policy, which has been in budget surplus for many years and government debt is only 7 per cent of GDP. Luxembourg also retained a 'monetary institute' to issue its currency, although monetary policy under the union was effectively run by Belgium.

Luxembourg is an entirely open economy with exports consituting 93 per cent of GDP. Most of this represents trade with Belgium, and trade figures with the outside world are normally consolidated for the two countries. The economy is clearly dominated by that of Belgium, but has occasionally gone its own way: for example, GDP grew strongly in the early 1990s when the rest of Europe, including Belgium, was in recession. Inflation has normally been similar, but not identical, to that of Belgium but unemployment has traditionally been virtually non-existent, and is still only 2.4 per cent, less than one-third that of Belgium.

This is an example of monetary union on the lines of EMU, with two countries under one currency and one monetary policy but operating as separate political entities with separate fiscal policies. This was clearly sustainable for a long period, and points to a successful precedent for EMU. However, it must be acknowledged that it operated under very special circumstances. Given its small size, Luxembourg must be regarded as merely an appendage to the Belgian economy, much the same as Belgium itself is to Germany. Consequently, it has been an easy path to follow, given the additional benefits of proximity and a shared language. It would be wrong to conclude that countries of more equal size, and more disparate structures, can form a monetary union quite as easily.

UK AND IRELAND

A similar system operated between the UK and Ireland for many years, until the Irish pound joined the EMS in 1979. The Irish state achieved independence from the UK in 1922, and from 1927 began to issue its own coins, with a one-to-one link with sterling, which remained legal tender in Ireland. A central bank was established in Ireland in 1943, but monetary policy essentially followed that of the Bank of England. The economy was dominated by the UK, although the extent of this gradually lessened as Irish trade increased with other countries. In 1926 the UK took 97 per cent of Irish exports; by 1979 it was down to 50 per cent. However, the economy remained very much in tune with that of the UK and interest rates closely followed developments in the sterling market.

This was a similar situation to that of Belgium–Luxembourg, with separate political entities, separate fiscal policies, but effectively one monetary policy and one currency. A major difference was that Ireland increasingly began to move away from the UK and exert its own independence, but until 1979 the system operated smoothly and efficiently.

However, this was another combination of very favourable circumstances. During the period of monetary union Irish GDP was only some 3–4 per cent of that of the UK. The mobility of labour between the two has always been extremely high. Again, it is easy for such a system to work if one economy is merely an appendage to a much larger one.

OTHER RECENT MONETARY UNIONS

Other recent examples which may be cited included the short-lived East African Currency Union, which comprised Kenya, Uganda and Tanzania from shortly after independence in 1967 until 1977. These countries remained separate politically, with their own separate central banks, and, as might have been expected from looking at previous examples, the union quickly broke down.

By contrast, the East Caribbean Currency Area, similarly formed by six tiny islands after independence in 1965, still survives. This has the advantage of one central bank to manage the East Caribbean dollar across the whole area despite the islands remaining as separate political entities with their own fiscal policies. Their small size and relative isolation perhaps explains its continued existence.

Finally, the 'Franc des Colonies Françaises d'Afrique' (known as the CFA franc) has survived for some forty years, being a currency union of old French colonies fixed against the French franc. This is a system that has been entirely managed and guaranteed by the Bank of France and thus does not really constitute a monetary union in its own right. Under EMU, the CFA franc will remain fixed against the euro and will continue to be managed by the Bank of France.

GERMAN RE-UNIFICATION

The most recent example of monetary union, until EMU itself, followed the collapse of the Eastern bloc, which resulted in the political re-unification of East and West Germany in 1990. This involved the merging into West Germany of an economy, as measured in population terms, of about 25 per cent its size. In principle this should not have proved as troublesome as it transpired, since even though East Germany was run down and inefficient compared with the West, it was at least a re-unificaton of the same nation.

Unfortunately, two developments conspired to create problems. First, the government (overruling the advice of the Bundesbank) converted the East German Mark into the Deutschmark at a rate of one to one. A more realistic rate, reflecting the respective competitivity of the two economies, would have been four or five to one. This rendered the bulk of East Germany's industrial capacity initially uncompetitive. Secondly, nominal wages in the East, which were only some 50 per cent of levels of the West in 1990, were rapidly pushed up towards Western levels, reaching some 75 per cent within only three years and continuing to rise thereafter. This reflected pressures by trade unions in the West to prevent cheap labour from the East flooding across and bringing their members' wages down. Unfortunately, since labour productivity in the East was only some 30 per cent of Western levels, this meant that the East remained vastly uncompetitive.

Since then adjustment to the monetary union has been slow. Despite massive subsidies from the West, labour productivity in the East is still around half of Western levels and unemployment twice as high. Labour has flowed from East to West, but not in the large numbers that might have been expected to even out productivity and employment. The problem will doubtless be resolved eventually, but the whole process will take much longer than it should have done.

This episode offers some salutary lessons for EMU. First, rapid equalization of wages across EMU would be very damaging to areas that suffer from low productivity, which basically means many of the regions in

> *Rapid equalization of wages across EMU would be very damaging to areas that suffer from low productivity.*

southern Europe, some of which have productivity levels not much above East Germany's. Secondly, labour has been suprisingly slow to move from East to West (around 7 per cent of the former East population has moved to the West since unification), despite being part of the same nation. This bodes ill for labour mobility across the different countries of EMU. Thirdly, the heavy cost of monetary unification has been borne by the West, not without a good deal of discontent by taxpayers, but would this cost have been acceptable without the irreversible fact of political union?

IMPLICATIONS FOR EMU

Comparing EMU with the events of the past, particularly those of the nineteenth century, may be somewhat difficult given the much changed structure of the world economy today. The world of 150 years ago incorporated a more rudimentary financial system based on precious-metal coinage. Central banking was somewhat basic. But it was also a period of high migratory flows, greater wage and price flexibility, and much lower government involvement in economic activity, which are all factors that should have assisted the stabilization of exchange rates rather than hindered them.

The lessons for EMU from the past are that sustained monetary union has tended to occur under two types of conditions.

First, when monetary union is preceded by political union as in the examples of Germany and Italy. It is true that nineteenth-century German unification followed a similar path to EMU, having begun as a customs union, but it would probably not have developed into full monetary union without the political activities of Bismarck. Political union is a necessary prerequisite for monetary union, it could be argued, in order that the large adjustment costs of it become acceptable, as in the case of German re-unification in the 1990s. The long process of centralization of monetary union would not have been achieved in Italy and the US without political union. Also, the Latin and Scandinavian monetary unions eventually floundered without political union to support them.

Second, monetary union has been shown to have survived, along the lines of EMU, in situations wherein a locally dominant economy takes a much smaller satellite along with it, as in the cases of Belgium/Luxembourg and the UK/Ireland. German monetary union was also made much easier in the 1870s by the dominance of Prussia, whose state bank was transformed into the German national bank. This would imply for EMU that a union of Germany with, say, Belgium, Netherlands and Austria would function smoothly, but the introduction of other large states such as France, Italy and Spain is a much more challenging undertaking.

However, we should add an important caveat. It is apparent in analyzing EMU from a historical perspective that nothing quite like it has actually occurred before. In previous examples monetary union has been enforced as a result of the tide of historical events that have brought about political union. Previous attempts at monetary union of separate countries, such as the Latin Monetary Union, were half-hearted affairs that involved members still retaining their own central banks and monetary independence. But under EMU a group of states have voluntarily renounced monetary independence in order to jointly form a much larger currency area. Whether or not this does indeed require, or inevitably lead to, closer political union remains to be seen.

Part

3

ECONOMIC PERSPECTIVE

Part 3 will provide the theoretical building blocks which are necessary to evaluate EMU from a purely economic point of view. Chapter 8 discusses the development of the basic theory of monetary unions. The following chapter puts this analysis in the context of economic events over the last thirty years, and describes the evolving theoretical framework which has underpinned the movement towards EMU. Chapter 10 will draw the separate strands of thought together and summarize the fundamental economic factors that we should look at in order to evaluate the likely success of EMU.

Chapter 8

··

THE BASIC CRITERIA FOR AN OPTIMUM CURRENCY AREA

The economic analysis of monetary union aims to assess the criteria by which a given country decides whether or not it should give up maintaining its own exchange rate in favour of being part of a larger exchange rate regime. An exchange rate regime that fulfils these criteria is deemed to be an 'optimum currency area'. In other words, it is efficient in achieving the goals of economic equilibrium, which are normally defined as full employment and price stability.

This branch of economic analysis is relatively recent considering the long history of economic thought. The debate over the relative merits of fixed versus flexible exchange rates has taxed economists for many years. However, in 1961 the Canadian economist Robert Mundell considered a more fundamental question, namely what size of economic area should maintain its own separate currency. This article first coined the phrase 'optimum currency area' (Mundell, 1961). In Part 3 we will consider the early formulation of this theory and discuss how it has been modified over the years.

Before considering what makes a currency area an optimum one, we will outline the several choices a country has in deciding which exchange rate system it should adopt. These are as follows:

1 A freely floating exchange rate.

2 An exchange rate fixed but adjustable against a reference currency (or basket of currencies). This system prevailed for the post-1945 period until the early 1970s, when most world currencies were fixed against the US dollar.

3 An exchange rate permanently fixed against a reference currency but the domestic central bank continues to issue its own money. An example would be the 'currency board' system operated by some countries at present (such as the fixing of the Hong Kong dollar against the US dollar). In this system the issue of domestic money must be fully backed by reserves of the reference currency. Although similar in some ways to monetary union this allows deviation in domestic interest rates from that of the reference currency.

4 Full monetary union, or integration, in which responsibility for the creation of money, the setting of interest rates, and exchange rate management are passed over to a union-wide central bank. This is the type of arrangement now existing in Europe.

By joining a full monetary union, certain advantages are immediately gained. These are primarily as follows:

- The elimination of currency transaction costs on intra-union trade. Companies no longer have to pay currency spreads, maintain foreign exchange departments or incur hedging costs on such trade.

- Greater price certainty throughout the union area. With all goods priced in the same currency, it is much easier to compare the prices of the same good across different countries. Currency union should thus ensure a more efficient working of the economic system.

These benefits are fairly self-evident. What is more difficult to assess are the costs involved in joining a currency union, due to the loss of the exchange rate as an independent policy instrument. Evaluating these costs forms the core of the economic analysis of currency unions.

Even though these ideas were only formulated some forty years ago, the following outlines what may be termed the basic or 'traditional' criteria for joining a currency area.

What is difficult to assess are the costs involved in joining a currency union.

FACTOR MOBILITY

This was the issue on which Mundell's classic article focused, namely the extent to which the factors used to produce economic output were mobile across the currency area. Since the most important factor of production is labour, this effectively becomes a question of the structure of the labour market.

This analysis is most easily explained by examining what happens in the event of an economic disturbance that results in an excess supply of labour (i.e., rise in unemployment) within one of a group of countries trading together.

(a) Factor mobility under conditions of labour market flexibility

Consider, for example, the effect of a sudden fall in the demand for exports from Belgium. This causes a rise in unemployment in that country. If wages are flexible in Belgium, unemployment causes them to fall. This would induce an outflow of the surplus labour from Belgium to other countries in Europe where demand for labour remains strong. The removal of surplus labour in Belgium subsequently bids wages there back up to previous levels, thus restoring equilibrium in the labour market. This is illustrated in Figure 8.1.

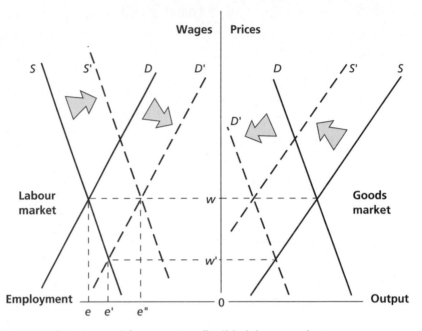

Fig 8.1. Fall in demand for exports – flexible labour market

1 The right hand panel shows demand and supply curves for Belgian output; the left hand panel show the resulting demand and supply curves for Belgian labour.
2 A fall in demand for Belgian goods causes the demand curve in the goods market to shift from D to D'. This causes a corresponding shift in the demand curve in the labour market from D to D'. This causes employment to fall from e to e' and wages from w to w'.
3 If labour is mobile, the downward pressure on wages causes labour to move abroad. The reduced supply of labour causes downward shifts in the Belgian supply curves for goods and labour from S to S'. This goes on until wages are re-established at their old level of w, with employment at the even lower level of e".
4 If labour fails to move abroad after the fall in demand, the labour supply curve remains at S and wages at w'. However, the resulting lower price of Belgian output eventually causes the demand curve for output, and hence labour, to shift back to their original positions at D, thus returning wages to w.

It may be of course that labour is not as mobile as this between countries. The emergence of surplus labour in Belgium may simply cause Belgian wages to fall relative to the rest of Europe, while higher unemployment continues to prevail, because labour fails to move abroad. However, there is still an automatic return to full employment. The much lower costs now prevailing in Belgium cause a rise in demand for its exports to the rest of Europe. Thus eventually its surplus labour is re-absorbed into employment and wages move back up to previous levels. What happens by comparison with the previous example is that exchange of labour is replaced by the exchange of goods, but the result is the same (this is also illustrated in Fig. 8.1). In both cases equilibrium is restored without the Belgian exchange rate having to move.

(b) Factor mobility under conditions of labour market inflexibility

In the above case, problems resolve themselves because of the efficient working of the labour market, the prime requirement being that wages are flexible. However, it was a major precept of macro-economics, first formulated by Keynes in the 1930s, that the price of labour, i.e., wages, tended to be inflexible downwards. This occurred because of institutional rigidities, such as minimum wage legislation or trade union power. Returning to the example, this would mean that wages do not fall in Belgium so that there would be no incentive for the surplus to flow abroad. Nor can there be any resolution to the problem by increased exports since there is no cost advantage relative to the rest of Europe. The result is simply continued high Belgian unemployment (*see* Fig. 8.2).

In this case, the desirability for an exchange rate adjustment becomes apparent. Belgium can devalue its currency, thus establishing a cost advantage versus other countries. Demand for its products rises and unemployment is removed.

What essentially happens in this case is that the currency adjustment compensates for the fact that wages do not fall in response to excess labour supply. Wages in Belgium have not changed but the lower Belgian exchange rate causes them to fall in terms of foreign currency. It is the fall in wages in terms of foreign currency that restores equilibrium in the labour market by stimulating demand from abroad. Thus the same result is achieved as in the previous

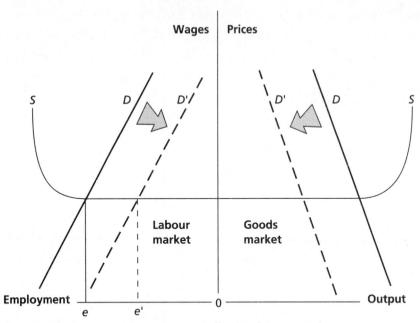

Fig 8.2 Fall in demand for exports – inflexible labour market

1 The right hand panel shows the demand and supply curves for Belgian output; the left hand panel shows demand and supply curves for Belgian labour. In this case, the labour supply curve (and hence the goods supply curve) becomes horizontal at lower wage levels reflecting the downward inflexibility of wages.
2 A fall in demand for Belgian goods from abroad causes both demand curves to shift down from *D* to *D'*. But wages and prices do not fall, so employment simply declines from *e* to *e'*.
3 If Belgium devalued the franc, wages and prices in foreign currency terms are reduced. Hence demand curves shift back to *D*, and employment is restored to its former level at *e*.

example, where full employment was restored by the fall in domestic nominal wages without the need for an exchange rate change.

The implications for optimum currency areas are clear. In the case of (a), the labour market is sufficiently flexible such that exchange rate adjustment is unnecessary. There would be no costs to Belgium forming a currency union with the rest of Europe. In the case of (b), a currency union would be inefficient, since currency adjustment is needed to restore balance in the labour market. Significant costs to joining a union could appear in the form of persistent unemployment.

This analysis can be equally applied to an existing monetary union. Suppose that a region suffered from an excess supply of labour due to a fall in demand for its product. An example might be the recession in Texas in the 1980s due to the fall in the demand for the region's local product, oil. Since there is no exchange rate to change, the excess labour must move elsewhere, or local nominal wages fall. It may be argued that on this particular occasion it would have been easier for the Texan economy to have returned to full employment by having its own currency and devaluing.

This analysis thus concludes that an optimum currency area should be defined as one over which labour moves freely, i.e., over which the labour market was efficient. It was assumed at the time that this theory was formulated (in the early 1960s) that labour markets were generally extremely inefficient, primarily due to the downward inflexibility of wages. In addition, currency markets were dominated by the exchange of goods and services at this time and capital flows were relatively small. Governments could therefore control exchange rates relatively easily, and the exchange rate was seen as a major policy 'tool' to counter inefficiencies in the economy's price mechanism.

OPENNESS OF THE ECONOMY

An early refinement of this analysis pointed to the fact that economies are not all of an equivalent size or structure (McKinnon, 1963). In some economies ('open' economies) external trade is a much higher proportion of overall economic activity than others ('closed' economies). An example of an open economy would be Belgium, where external trade constitutes some

Economies are not all of an equivalent size or structure.

65 per cent of GDP, and an example of a closed economy would be

the United States, where trade constitutes only 12 per cent of GDP. It is also apparent from these examples that open economies tend to be small and closed economies tend to be large.

The introduction of 'openness' as a factor means that we must recognize that there are essentially two types of goods in the economy. These are 'traded' goods, such as manufactured products, which are exchanged internationally, and 'non-traded' goods, such as most services, which cannot move from one country to another. The prices of traded goods are determined in world markets and thus taken as 'fixed' by any one country, while the prices of non-traded goods are determined by domestic economic factors, which basically means the level of domestic wages.

Consideration of openness indicated that the usefulness of an exchange rate adjustment as a policy instrument was markedly different for the two types of economy. This occurs primarily because in a small open economy a devaluation has a major subsequent effect on domestic prices, and hence domestic wage levels, whereas in a closed economy it does not (*see* Box 8.1).

BOX 8.1

Impact of exchange rate changes in open and closed economies

Consider the effects of an expansion of domestic demand in Belgium, with the economy near to full employment, and with an initially unchanged exchange rate. A rise in demand causes excess spending across the whole economy. The bulk of this falls on the traded goods sector, because of its dominant size. But in this sector prices are determined in world markets and are not affected by the rise in spending in one particular country. The immediate result is a sharp deterioration in the trade balance as goods are drawn in from abroad to satisfy the excess domestic demand.

If the same expansion of domestic demand occurs in the US, however, the bulk of the excess demand falls on the large non-traded goods sector, and is absorbed initially in the form of higher prices rather than a trade deficit.

▶

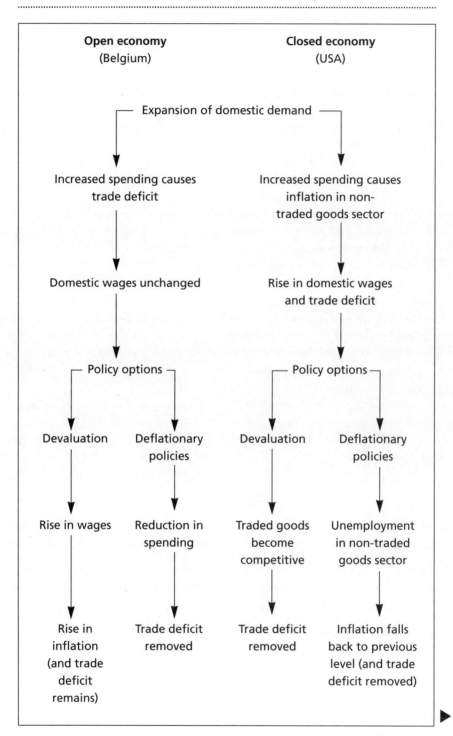

Open economy (Belgium)	Closed economy (USA)

Expansion of domestic demand

Increased spending causes trade deficit	Increased spending causes inflation in non-traded goods sector

Domestic wages unchanged	Rise in domestic wages and trade deficit

Policy options — Policy options

Devaluation	Deflationary policies	Devaluation	Deflationary policies

Rise in wages	Reduction in spending	Traded goods become competitive	Unemployment in non-traded goods sector

Rise in inflation (and trade deficit remains)	Trade deficit removed	Trade deficit removed	Inflation falls back to previous level (and trade deficit removed)

▶

Compare now the appropriate policy response in these two examples. In the case of Belgium we have inflationary pressure manifested in the form of a trade deficit, and consequent downward pressure on the exchange rate. If the authorities decide to devalue, a higher inflation rate is immediately transmitted to the whole economy. This happens because of the dominant size of the traded goods sector, which causes factor prices (i.e. wages) to rise in response to the highly visible rise in traded goods prices. The result of the exercise is simply higher overall prices in Belgian franc terms. A more appropriate policy response for Belgium would be the implementation of deflationary monetary and fiscal policies to remove the excess demand and restore equilibrium at the existing exchange rate.

In the case of the US, by contrast, we have a situation of inflation already having established itself within the non-traded goods sector, which is quickly transmitted into higher wages. Higher wages subsequently render the traded goods sector uncompetitive in world markets. In this case a depreciation of the currency would restore the competitivity of factor prices, in effect recognizing the inflation that has already taken place. The implementation of deflationary policies to maintain the existing exchange rate would, by contrast, involve the unemployment of resources in the large non-traded goods sector in order to to restore the viability of the small traded goods sector.

The conclusion to be drawn is that the exchange rate is a much more efficient policy instrument for closed economies than it is for open economies.

This appears at first sight to be an unnecessarily complicated piece of analysis, but it is crucial in understanding how different economies behave with respect to the exchange rate. The important point is the relative sizes of the traded and non-traded sectors (i.e., the degree of openness). In the case of a closed economy, such as the US, prices of domestic factors of production (i.e., wages) are determined by the non-traded goods sector. Currency depreciation can restore the competitivity of the traded goods sector without necessarily causing further inflation of wages. By contrast, in the case of an open economy, such as Belgium, domestic wage levels are dominated by the prices of traded goods established in world markets – currency depreciation just causes inflation and the exchange rate is thus not useful as a policy tool.

Clearly, the loss of the exchange rate has less significance for open economies so that they are better candidates for joining a monetary union than closed economies.

COMMON INFLATION RATE

The adoption of a common currency between two or more economic areas means that not only can the exchange rate no longer be used as a policy tool but also member countries cannot operate independent monetary policies, as interest rates will be set by a union-wide central bank. A problem arises, therefore, if the trade-off between inflation and unemployment (i.e., lower inflation at the expense of higher unemployment) differs sharply between countries due to structural economic factors. Thus convergence of inflation rates ahead of monetary union, and the subsequent maintenance of zero differentials under permanently fixed exchange rates, may only be achieved at a much higher unemployment cost in one area versus another.

Monetary union is thus only desirable if it can be established that the political will exists, first, to maintain a given inflation rate target at whatever cost, and secondly, to surrender national autonomy of policy in achievement of this goal.

ECONOMIC DIVERSIFICATION

It makes sense for countries considering monetary union to be structurally alike. This greatly reduces the strain imposed on factors of production having to flow from one country to another in response to economic disturbances.

Accordingly, a requirement for monetary union specified in the early economic literature on the subject (Kenen, 1969) was that participating economies should be well-diversified. If each economy in the proposed union produces a wide variety of products, then a demand disturbance in any one industry would not unduly disrupt a particular member of the union (an 'asymmetric shock').

It makes sense for countries considering monetary union to be structurally alike.

For example, it may not be desirable for an economy based largely on the production of raw materials, such as Australia, to form a union with a country based on the production of manufactured goods. A large and prolonged drop in raw material prices would clearly promote excessive strains on one part of the union but not the other. Thus countries each with a well diversified, rather than a single product, economic base have less need for exchange rate flexibility between each other.

However, in purely theoretical terms, this criterion was seen as somewhat ambiguous. As trade between countries increases (as it will among monetary union members), the traditional economic theory of comparative advantage suggests that greater specialization should occur. If each country concentrates its resources in producing the good in which its factors of production are most efficient, so the theory goes, then overall output is maximized. Advantage can be taken of economies of scale. A paradox thus arises (not unusual in economic analysis), since if greater specialization occurs among members of a monetary union, this implies the need for an exchange rate to counter industry-specific shocks.

BASIC THEORY SUMMARIZED

The theory outlined above, mostly formulated in the 1960s and early 1970s, was generally hostile to the concept of monetary union. This was primarily a reflection of economic events at the time. Considering each of the above criteria in turn:

- Factor mobility: the world was generally regarded as full of wage and price rigidities, factors were immobile and exchange rate flexibility considered necessary to compensate for this.
- Economic openness: while small open economies such as Belgium and the Netherlands would be obvious candidates for monetary union on this criterion, for most economies the conclusion was not so clear cut. In fact, in the major economies of Europe (UK, France, Germany and Italy), the external sector stood between 14 per cent and 20 per cent of GDP in the 1960s. These were thus towards the closed end of the spectrum and it seemed much better for these countries to keep their own currencies.
- Common inflation rate: given extremely large and fluctuating inflation differentials across countries, particularly in the 1970s, the concept of inflation convergence seemed a distant likelihood, as each country sought its own inflation/unemployment trade-off.
- Economic diversification: if greater trade brought increased specialization, then this would not be conducive to monetary union. There was something of a paradox in this assessment that made the idea of monetary union questionable.

It was thus not suprising that Harry Johnson, one of the leading monetary economists of the time, wrote in 1969 that consideration of currency areas was a 'dead end problem' and that 'it seems to me unlikely that any further major theoretical breakthroughs can be made within the confines of the optimum currency area concept' (Johnson, 1969).

Chapter 9

THE SHIFTING ECONOMIC LANDSCAPE

Economic theory has a way of following events in the real world. Countries' economic structures change and previously held precepts go by the board as new theories need to be devised to explain actual economic developments. Hence some of the initial thinking about optimum currency areas has had to be modified somewhat in recent years. This has resulted in a more favourable view of the desirability of monetary union. The political movement towards the implementation of EMU itself has thus been accompanied by developments in economic theory justifying it.

FACTOR MOBILITY

The disinflation of the 1980s, and more particularly the 1990s, suggested that wages were not as downwardly inflexible as previously thought. This was accompanied by the observation of a diminution of union power in some countries and a resurrection of the significance of market forces. In terms of theory, this was rationalized by the development of labour market theories to explain the downward 'stickiness' of wages. These included the introduction of the role of price expectations in setting wages, the nature of wage contracts and the effect of imperfect market information. Thus wages came to be seen as inflexible only in the short term due to the dynamics of the free market, rather than fundamentally inflexible over the long term due to institutional factors. This would suggest less need for currency adjustment to circumvent price rigidities.

This viewpoint should perhaps be qualified slightly. The reduction of world inflation from its high around 1980 actually took a considerable number of years to achieve, mainly because inflationary expectations tend to be revised down only slowly. Moreover, whatever may be rationalized by complicated theoretical models, it is an observed fact that labour markets in some countries (such as the US or Asia) are considerably more flexible than others (such as Europe). Whether or not the European labour markets are flexible enough to justify monetary union can only be established by examining the empirical evidence in the countries concerned (to be discussed in a subsequent chapter). But, in general, in a world where actual deflation is now a real prospect in some countries, prices and wages are seen as more flexible than they were twenty or so years ago.

> *Whether or not the European labour markets are flexible enough to justify monetary union can only be established by examining the empirical evidence in the countries concerned.*

New theories have also emerged to explain labour mobility. One of the most important is that labour mobility is a function of uncertainty (Bertola, 1989). The argument is that the more certain is an expected stream of potential income from a different job, the more labour is likely to relocate to another area in search of one. In terms of labour moving between countries, a major degree of uncertainty is the exchange rate. Thus it may be argued that the removal of exchange rate barriers will automatically make labour more mobile across Europe. Again some qualification is in order since other factors must also affect labour mobility – otherwise the sharp regional differentials in previously existing currency areas, such as between the north and south of Italy, would not have persisted.

OPENNESS OF THE ECONOMY

This concept has remained valid although it has been reformulated in terms of a country's ability to influence its 'real' exchange rate. This measures the extent to which any fall in a country's exchange rate is reflected in its subsequent wage and price level. If it causes a one-for-one rise in domestic prices, then clearly it is impossible to change the real exchange rate at all, in which case there is no point in maintaining a separate exchange rate to adjust.

This, it is now argued, is increasingly the case in Europe, where wage indexation is more prevalent than in the US. Moreover, European economies have steadily been becoming more open, as trade between each other has increased. Exports in France and Italy, for example, now stand at nearly 25 per cent of GDP compared with around 14 per cent in the 1960s. Thus, 'real' exchange rate adjustment is becoming less feasible. Again this is an empirical question as to how open an economy should be to warrant giving up its exchange rate, and the extent to which trade is conducted with other union members.

COMMON INFLATION RATE

It has become clear that the traditional concept of a straightforward trade-off in each country between inflation and unemployment represented something of a simplification. This followed from the observation during the 1970s that in most countries inflation and unemployment steadily rose together. It became clear that there was no obvious trade-off between the two and unemployment instead gravitated inexorably towards its fundamental long-term rate (*see* Box 9.1).

Although the connection between this analysis and monetary union is not immediately obvious, it actually has important implications. One of the potential costs to a country from joining a

---

| BOX 9.1 |

Trade-off between inflation and unemployment

In theoretical terms this was explained by the 'natural' rate of unemployment concept (Friedman, 1968 and Phelps, 1971), which became generally accepted by the beginning of the 1980s. This asserted that equilibrium in the labour market is determined in the long run entirely by structural (i.e., demographic and institutional) factors. The government cannot, therefore, choose its own desired unemployment rate and set its demand management policies accordingly to achieve it.

This theory is explained in Fig. 9.1, which shows the overall price inflation (*P*) on the vertical axis and unemployment (*U*) on the horizontal axis. Unemployment is initially in equilibrium at *u'* with price inflation at *p'*. Assume the government increases domestic demand to reduce unemployment in return for a little more inflation. Unemployment falls to *u"* and inflation rises to *p"*. But this only happens because wage inflation, represented by the curve *w'*, remains unchanged. Unemployment has gone down only because real wages have fallen.

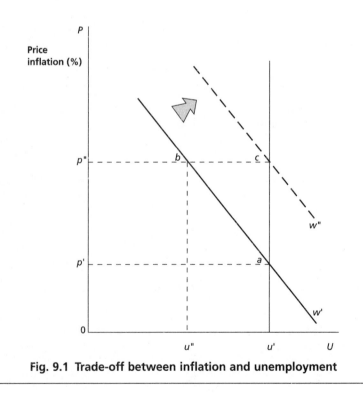

Fig. 9.1 Trade-off between inflation and unemployment

▶

This situation is only temporary. The higher price inflation eventually causes wage inflation to move up as well, which means that the *w* curve shifts upwards to *w"* and the economy ends up at point *c*. Real wages are thus back up to their previous levels and unemployment back at *u'*. There is no permanent trade-off between inflation and unemployment, which always reverts to its 'natural' rate at *u'*, and we just have higher inflation. The curve between inflation and unemployment is actually vertical.

monetary union, namely having to give up its desired unemployment rate in order to achieve the common inflation rate within the union, effectively disappears. Thus over the long term, if this theory is correct, the cost in terms of unemployment of having an inflation rate of, say, 2 per cent or 10 per cent is exactly the same.

It became painfully apparent during the 1970s that high and volatile inflation has very disruptive economic effects. Relative price movements within an economy are the means by which market information is transmitted and resources allocated. High inflation swamps and distorts relative price movements. Given this, it has been the choice of most European countries to move towards a low inflation rate, thus avoiding these distortions. This leads

The availability of an independent monetary policy and a flexible exchange rate merely gives a country the ability to choose its own inflation rate, and nothing more.

to a very important conclusion, namely that the availability of an independent monetary policy and a flexible exchange rate merely gives a country the ability to choose its own inflation rate, and nothing more. Since most countries now see the benefits of having inflation as low as possible, this choice is not really worth very much. The loss of an independent monetary policy in the context of a monetary union is thus now seen as much less important than previously.

But we should be careful not to overstate the case in this matter. In our view the 'natural' rate hypothesis is a valid one, and crucial in understanding the inflation process. However, it should not be used to argue that there can be no unemployment costs to monetary union at all. First, there is still an unemployment/inflation trade-off in the 'short term', which can run into years. Secondly, the natural rate itself is not a fixed point but tends to move around as demographic and technological factors change. For example, unemployment in the UK has recently fallen well below levels which in previous economic cycles have been associated with strong inflation. It is thus very difficult to know how near any particular country is to its natural rate at any one time. It is not necessarily true, therefore, that demand management policies should not be used to shift the unemployment rate at all.

We can conclude, therefore, that the potential costs of joining monetary union from each country giving up its own independent monetary policy are now much lower, but have by no means disappeared.

ECONOMIC DIVERSIFICATION

The idea that increased trade will necessarily lead to greater industrial specialization has been questioned. While it is true that considerations of economies of scale should lead to greater industrial concentration under a monetary union, there is no reason why this concentration should be confined, *post* monetary union, within any particular national boundary. Furthermore, it has been observed that much of European trade is intra-industry (i.e., within the same industry) rather than inter- (between different) industries. Figures produced by the OECD have shown a remarkable increase in intra-industry trade in manufactured goods in Europe over the last thirty years (OECD, 1994).

If union members do continue to enjoy a broad spectrum of industries, the requirement for labour market flexibility to respond to specific industry shocks is much reduced. In the example given in Figures 8.1 and 8.2, a sudden fall in demand for Belgium's exports alone is unlikely to occur if the rest of Europe produces a similar mix of output. If the steel industry, for example, is depressed in Belgium, it will probably be depressed in the rest of Europe, so that an exchange rate response would not be appropriate. The exchange rate affects the whole economy and thus if it is used at all should be used for economy-wide purposes rather than for specific industries.

This leads us to the question of how far union members should experience similarity in their overall economic cycles. It has become apparent in Europe that greater trade with each other has resulted in the emergence of a more definitive European economic cycle over the last 15 years (with some notable exceptions, such as the UK). This suggests that the exchange rate is becoming less necessary as a policy tool for these economies. Clearly, such convergence is crucial as the same interest rate policy is now applied to all countries under monetary union.

There is a further aspect to this question of economic similarity, or convergence. This relates to each country's productivity, i.e., output per man-hour. It is apparent that major differentials in productivity levels exist from country to country. If wages were quickly equalized across a monetary union, then a country suffering from low productivity would not be able to sell its goods in the rest of the area. Thus when we talk of 'economic convergence' between union members we have to consider productivity levels as well.

OPERATION OF THE FOREIGN EXCHANGE MARKET

Since 1973 the world monetary system has operated under a system of flexible exchange rates. This has seen periods of extreme and unpredictable movement. As experience of this regime built up, one fact became clearly apparent. This was that currency values were no longer determined by the flow of international trade in goods, as in traditional economic theory, but by movements in financial capital.

Accordingly, new theories needed to be developed to explain how currencies behaved. This introduced the asset market approach to currencies (*see*, for example, Dornbusch, 1976), which basically runs as follows. A currency is regarded as a financial asset, rather like an individual company's stock, and a currency's price (i.e., its exchange rate) is that at which the market is prepared to hold the existing supply of it. The currency markets are dominated by expectations and the price of each currency fluctuates as market views on the country concerned change. Being an asset market, a currency is often subject to volatile movements, and occasionally considerable overshooting, before a new equilibrium level is found. The massive rise and fall of the US dollar in the mid-1980s is the most dramatic example of such behaviour.

This change in the nature of currency markets has the following implications for the theory of optimum currency areas:

(a) Additional costs to maintaining a separate currency

These are:

- A currency may be subject to unpredictable speculative attacks, unrelated to developments in the real economy. Traditional theory confined itself to consideration of real economic disturbances in the context of monetary union, but monetary disturbances are clearly also significant. By joining a common currency these disturbances are much reduced (Bofinger, 1994).
- High currency volatility undermines the liquidity value of money. It is stability in value that gives money its liquidity, i.e., its acceptability as a means of payment. The more exchange rates fluctuate, the more this is eroded. Clearly, this is a greater problem for open

economies, where currency instability causes more fluctuation in the overall price level, than in closed economies.

- Given the high degree of financial integration in Europe, it is possible that the implementation of monetary policy is more appropriate at Europe-wide than at country level. For example, it may well be easier to control money supply growth for the whole of Europe rather than for individual countries.

(b) More limited use of the exchange rate as a policy tool

If currencies are determined primarily by financial capital flows, it becomes less feasible to use the exchange rate as a policy tool to influence the real economy. It is now much more difficult for the authorities to actually move the exchange rate to a desired level. This became painfully apparent during the 1992–3 ERM crisis. This involved the humiliating ejection of sterling and the lira from the system, and the decision to expand the ERM exchange rate bands to a ludicrously wide 15 per cent. This was tacit acceptance by the authorities that exchange rate markets were too powerful to be controlled.

In such markets, currency devaluation is not a flexible instrument that can be used frequently. It embodies strong expectational effects, in the sense that once used currency market participants may begin to anticipate that it will be used again. If these expectations also begin

The more often devaluation is used, the less effective it becomes.

to permeate the labour market, then devaluation tends increasingly to be reflected in higher nominal wages, thus offsetting the desired impact on competitivity (i.e., it is more and more difficult to influence the real exchange rate).

This implies that the more often devaluation is used, the less effective it becomes. As discussed above, this is chiefly a function of the degree of openness of the economy, but as economic participants become increasingly rational, devaluation becomes less and less effective irrespective of openness.

We should, however, provide some qualification to these arguments. Although currencies are dominated now by capital flows and strong expectational elements, these expectations are themselves primarily based on real economic criteria. For example, in the long run currencies still move broadly in line with inflation rate differentials. The asset market approach to currency movements is certainly valid, but participants still review the economic realities of a country before deciding whether or not to invest in the asset.

TIME CONSISTENCY AND CREDIBILITY

A new set of arguments in the context of currency unions relates to the consistency and credibility of national governments. It is argued that some potential currency union members have large credibility gains to be made from joining up with traditionally low inflation countries (Tavlas, 1993). Market participants are aware that countries with a regular tendency to run high inflation rates have a temptation to renege on their inflation targets. This is because inflation is basically a tax (forcing taxpayers into higher tax brackets and thus enhancing government revenues). Indeed, it is a major source of revenue in inefficient tax systems. Thus governments in these countries have no 'time consistency' because inflation targets are unlikely to be met. Inflationary expectations within the economy are accordingly very slow to be brought down.

An obvious example is Italy. However, if Italy is part of a monetary union with Germany, it automatically inherits the low inflation credibility of the Bundesbank, with immediate gains in the form of lower inflationary expectations, lower long-term interest rates, and lower costs of servicing debt. Thus, it is argued that these gains need to be quantified for such countries when considering the desirability of monetary union. Indeed, this explains Italy's desperate desire to be included in EMU at the outset.

It should be acknowledged, however, that monetary union must also entail a countervailing cost for the low inflation countries: there must be losses accruing to Germany from watering down its inflation credibility by forming a union with Italy. It is not necessarily true that the union as a whole will maintain the low inflation credibility of its strongest member. A further problem with this argument is that it is not really a valid criterion for deciding if a country should participate in monetary union. On this basis, any country with high inflation may want to form a union with Germany to benefit from its low inflation. Moreover, the structural factors that traditionally have brought Italy higher inflation than elsewhere may reappear in monetary union in the form of higher Italian unemployment.

Chapter 10

OVERALL EVALUATION

Re-consideration of the basic theory of optimum currency areas, in the light of economic events over the last twenty years or so, has brought a more favourable view to the concept of monetary union. The idea of a 'cost' to monetary union by the loss of the ability to select a chosen inflation/unemployment mix has become less significant. In addition, the exchange rate itself is now seen as less useful as a policy tool for influencing economic activity, given the more complex nature of currency movements now apparent.

But it is clear from the above discussion that the fundamental precepts regarding the criteria for optimum currencies – namely labour market flexibility, trade structure and economic convergence – remain largely valid. Recent thinking represents essentially a shift of interpretation, plus a number of refinements, rather than a fundamentally different approach.

Much of the economic argument over monetary union reflects the fact that if monetary union takes place, some of the criteria are self-fulfilling, namely:

- Monetary union will bring greater trade between members and thus economic cycles of members should become more synchronized.
- Removal of currency risks reduces uncertainty and thus enhances labour mobility; if labour is mobile then monetary union is justified.
- Time consistency arguments indicate that some countries gain immediate anti-inflation credibility from participation in a union, thus ensuring their qualification on inflation grounds.

- Individual European economies are mainly (to varying degrees) open economies, but after monetary union Europe as a whole is now a closed economy, of a similar size and degree of openness as the United States and Japan.

A further confusion is that the costs of union are different according to whether or not we are looking at the long term or the short term. While it may be true that on purely theoretical grounds there is no long-term trade-off between inflation and unemployment, there clearly is a trade-off in the short term. The question is really one of how long it will take before factor mobility increases or economic cycles converge. If differences are considerable at the onset of monetary union, undue pressures on the system may cause a break-up of the project before sufficient convergence actually appears.

Recent refinements to the theory of optimum currency areas do not disguise the fact that there may be very real costs involved in the project over an extended period of time. Participation may not be appropriate for all countries and members need to be examined on a case-by-case basis.

To summarize the theoretical discussion, the main factors we should consider in deciding whether or not the European Union (or parts of it) qualifies as an optimum currency area are as follows:

Labour mobility

If labour is immobile and/or wages inflexible there will be costs to monetary union in the form of persistent localized unemployment.

Openness

More open economies are more suitable for union because:

- the large size of the external sector means that the benefits of union are greater, namely savings on transaction costs and enhanced price certainty

- the size of the tradeable goods sector also makes currency adjustment less useful
- the gains from being insulated from currency market shocks are greater.

Economic convergence

Countries should join together in monetary union if their economies have converged in the following areas:

- spread of industrial activity
- levels of labour productivity
- common economic cycle

It is apparent that little of this was contained in the convergence criteria of the Maastricht Treaty, which concentrated on inflation and interest rates, budget deficits and government debt. The theoretical outline we have developed suggests that it would have been appropriate to have included labour mobility,

The place of fiscal policy lies in minimizing the costs of union.

openness and commonality of economic cycles, rather than the excessive concentration on fiscal matters. The place of fiscal policy lies in minimizing the costs of union, which arise in the form of higher unemployment in some members, rather than as the main criterion for entry itself.

MONETARY AND FISCAL POLICY UNDER EMU

To evaluate the progress of economic and monetary union, it is important to have a basic understanding of the mechanics of economic policy under the new regime. Part 4 therefore explains how monetary and fiscal policy will operate under EMU and also looks at some of the potential problems that may arise in the early years.

Chapter 11

MONETARY POLICY

A centralized monetary policy is at the core of economic and monetary union. The adoption of a single currency throughout the participating countries obviates any need for individually determined interest rates and national monetary policy has therefore devolved to the European Central Bank (ECB). The ECB's ability to run a successful monetary policy will be determined by two factors: its operational framework and the extent to which a change in monetary conditions produces a uniform effect in the participating countries.

USING THE BUNDESBANK AS A ROLE MODEL

When casting around for a model on which to base the new European Central Bank, it is not surprising that the authorities took for their example the Bundesbank, which is widely regarded as Europe's most successful central bank.

The Bundesbank's operational framework has been shaped by the country's economic experiences in the first half of the twentieth century. Germany suffered two disastrous episodes of hyperinflation while monetary policy was under the jurisdiction of the politicians and, consequently, when setting up the Bundesbank's constitution, it was decided that the central bank should be allowed to operate independently of political influence. So unlike, for example, the US Federal Reserve Bank, it is not answerable to the government. Neither does it publish minutes of the proceed-

---

| BOX 11.1 |

Monetary policy versus fiscal policy

Economists have debated for decades on the relative effectiveness of monetary and fiscal policy. Monetary policy adjusts a country's economic activity through changes in interest rates while fiscal policy effects changes through government spending and taxation. The broad conclusion tends to be that fiscal measures have an immediate impact (i.e., within six months) but that they are relatively short-lived. Monetary policy, on the other hand, takes longer to work through the economy but, when the impact does eventually feed through, it is more powerful. Implementing monetary policy is rather like steering an ocean liner; a very small adjustment is needed well in advance to effect a smooth change in direction. For example, the German central bank's skill at running a stable and pre-emptive monetary policy has been a major contributing factor to the country's post-war economic success. By comparison, the UK has operated a rather more volatile monetary policy over the same period which has resulted in a somewhat erratic stop–go economic performance.

Under EMU, the effects of monetary policy are likely to be even more pronounced. With the EMU bloc now effectively one large, closed economy, in which trade with outside countries represents only about 13 per cent of GDP, economic activity will be more affected by domestic policy than by economic events outside the area.

---

ings of its policy-setting council. Despite this lack of 'openness', the Bundesbank would argue that its monetary policy is 'transparent' in that the public understands its goals and the reasons behind its interest rate decisions.

THE ECB'S OPERATIONAL FRAMEWORK

The ECB operates along broadly similar lines to the Bundesbank and, to underline its strong links with the German central bank, it is physically situated in Frankfurt. Policy is decided by a council which consists of an executive board – made up of a president, a vice-president and four members – and the 11 central bank governors of the participating countries. This split gives a bigger vote to the 'regional' input from the central bank governors (as opposed to the central executive) than either the Bundesbank, where 9 of the 17-strong council are regional representatives, or the US Federal Reserve, where only 5 of the 12 Federal Open Market Committee members are regional appointees. The ECB's independence is enshrined in the Maastricht Treaty, but there is concern that its strongly regional bias may render it susceptible to lobbying of national interests from the central bank governors rather than allowing it to take a broad overview of the eurozone as a whole.

The ECB is largely a decision-making body. National central banks of the EMU participants, which make up the European System of Central Banks (ESCB), still carry out the day-to-day money market and foreign exchange operations. They are also responsible for gathering and processing the mass of statistical information on which the ECB bases its interest rate decisions. This delineation of duties is reflected in the number of people working in the respective organizations. The Bundesbank and the Banque de France each employ over 10,000 people – whereas the ECB has a staff of only 500.

The national central banks also continue to undertake the role of financial supervision. In the event of a relatively small problem with a financial institution, it will be the responsibility of the central bank in whose jurisdiction the institution falls to organize a rescue operation. However, the IMF has warned that, under the present delineation of duties between the ECB and ESCB, *Although the Maastricht Treaty rules out the ECB acting as a lender of last resort, a major financial collapse would require an injection of liquidity.* there is some ambiguity about where the exact responsibility of lender of last resort will fall in the event of a major banking crisis.[1]

[1] *Financial Times*, 22 September 1998.

Although the Maastricht Treaty rules out the ECB acting as a lender of last resort, a major financial collapse would require an injection of liquidity (as happened in response to the 1987 stock market crash). This type of operation falls under the remit of monetary policy and would therefore have to be approved by the ECB.

The ECB's primary goal is the pursuit of price stability, with growth and employment secondary objectives. In order to achieve its inflation objective, the ECB needs to track specific indicators and use these as a financial barometer to give it early warning of when a change in monetary conditions is necessary. There are two different schools of thought about what the best indicator is for this purpose: one favours targeting money supply growth; and the other, inflation.

In the early 1980s great emphasis was placed on the relationship between growth in the money supply and the inflation rate and most central banks set a monetary target that then became the key arbiter in deciding when a change in interest rates was necessary. However, the direct relationship between money supply and inflation seemed to break down and even in Germany, where monetary targeting has generally been deemed a success, the Bundesbank has only met its target 50 per cent of the time. The reason for this is that the deregulation and structural changes that have occurred in the financial market place in recent years have changed people's pattern of financial behaviour. One of the effects of this has been to alter the speed at which money circulates around the economy – known as the velocity of circulation. The relationship between money supply and inflation only holds good if the velocity of circulation remains steady. As a result of the rather haphazard performance of monetary targeting, most central banks – apart from the Bundesbank – switched to targeting the inflation rate itself.

Probably due to its strong association with the Bundesbank, the ECB is known to favour still placing most emphasis on monetary targeting. However, unpredictable shifts in the demand for money in the aftermath of EMU are likely to mean that monetary statistics are somewhat unreliable. The ECB has therefore decided to use a three-pronged method of targeting to secure its inflation objective. The central prong is monetary targeting and to this end the ECB publishes annual monetary targets but, due to the uncertainty surrounding the quality of the monetary data, these will not be adhered to rigorously in the early years. A target inflation rate is also published, based on a harmonized index of consumer prices. In its first year of operation the ECB set this at 2 per cent or less. The third part of the prong is a mix of other indicators. The Bank's own ongoing forecasts (as opposed to their targets) for the rate of inflation and the mix of indicators are not made public and this essentially allows the ECB council to operate a more informal 'seat of the pants' approach. This flexibility might be necessary in the event of problems with the new aggregated economic data or any shifts in the relationship between economic variables.

There could also be some linkage between member governments' fiscal policy and the ECB's monetary policy. The president of the ECB, Wim Duisenberg, is known to be concerned that, after making such enormous strides in bringing government spending down towards the Maastricht limits, a number of countries are beginning to experience 'fiscal fatigue'.

This raises the question of how to reconcile a mismatch of monetary and fiscal policy in a system where monetary policy is centralized while fiscal policy remains decentralized. It is here that the problems of trying to harmonize policy with not just one government but eleven (and possible more in the future) are thrown into sharp relief. For example, what monetary policy adjustment will be made if a small country such as Belgium indulges in fiscal profligacy while France and Germany maintain a rigorous policy? It will be either, in monetary terms, a case of the tail wagging the dog or deciding to let some inflation occur in the peripheral economies.

Fashioning the ECB on the Bundesbank has the advantage of using a tried and tested formula – especially as the launch of EMU brings with it so many other economic and financial uncertainties. But the Bundesbank model has only worked well in Germany because, over the years, the Central Bank's success in keeping a tight control on inflation and maintaining the value of the Deutschmark has gradually earned it widespread public confidence. By setting a uniform monetary policy across the varied collection of EMU countries, the ECB faces a much harder task in establishing credibility with both the investment community and the public at large. Its task will be made more difficult by the fact that the ECB is adopting a mixed approach of monetary and inflation targeting. Furthermore, the decision to eschew an 'open' approach and rely instead on 'transparency' to justify its policy will increase the risk of a misunderstanding about what the ECB is seeking to do.

PROBLEMS WITH THE OPERATION OF EMU MONETARY POLICY

One-size monetary policy

Implementing a uniform monetary policy across a broad geographic and economic spread of countries is clearly more difficult than across a single country. The most obvious problem is that of an asymmetrical shock, i.e., one that is not experienced by other countries. Europe's experience in the early 1990s, as a result of German re-unification, exemplifies what can happen in a currency area if one country experiences an asymmetrical shock. The effects are much more widespread if it is the largest economy that receives the shock. But even when the shock is confined to a relatively small country or area (for example the impact of the collapse of communism on Finnish trade), the loss of control over interest rates and the exchange rate prevents a government from tailoring monetary policy to deal with the specific exigencies.

It is unlikely that there will be a shock as severe as that of the re-unification of Germany affecting one individual country but there could be severe problems adversely affecting a certain industry or region. There have been examples of this occurring in America – for example, the oil slump in the mid-1980s mentioned earlier which hit the state of Texas badly. But the US labour market is much more mobile and, with a federal budget amounting to 35.6 per cent of GDP compared to the EU's 1 per cent, there is also greater scope for the effects of any regional downturn to be mitigated by fiscal transfers from the central federal budget.

It is unlikely that there will be a shock as severe as that of the re-unification of Germany affecting one individual country.

Differing transmission mechanisms

The major problem, however, about operating a unilateral interest rate across the EMU countries is their differing 'transmission mechanisms' – this is the speed at which interest rate changes affect different economies. Interest rates impinge on economic activity in a number of different ways, such as the cost of capital and asset prices. One of the determinants of the extent to which interest rate changes impact on economic activity is the level of private sector debt in a country. Countries with a highly indebted private sector will be more severely affected by a given change in interest rates than countries where the private sector debt is lower. The structure of the private sector debt (whether it is at short-term, long-term, fixed or variable interest rates) is also an important factor. Clearly, the higher the proportion of variable rate debt, the more sensitive the economy is to interest rate changes.

According to an IMF Working Paper,[2] in respect of transmission

---

[2] 'The real effects of monetary policy in the European Union: what are the differences?' International Monetary Fund, Working Paper 997/160, December 1997.

of monetary policy, the EMU falls into two distinct groups. In France, Italy, Portugal and Spain, output takes only five to six quarters to bottom out after an episode of monetary tightening whereas in Austria, Belgium, Finland, Germany and the Netherlands it takes 11 to 12 quarters. Although an interest rate rise works its way through the economy more quickly in the first group, the resulting fall-off in economic activity is almost twice as pronounced in the second group.

Under EMU, there will eventually be a gradual harmonization of financial practices which is likely to result in the differing rates of transmission being ironed out. However, changing corporate finance practices and ownership structures will take some time and it could therefore be that the issue of differing transmission mechanisms presents the ECB with quite a problem, particularly in its early years.

Political conflict

Although the ECB's independence is guaranteed under the Maastricht Treaty, this does not mean that it is immune from political pressures. During the two years preceding the launch of EMU, Europe's political landscape tilted sharply to the left. The new left-of-centre governments are placing more emphasis on expansionary fiscal policies than their predecessors. Not only are these more likely to result in breaches of the stability pact, but there are also suggestions that the politicians should set the ECB an exchange rate target for the euro. The ECB have rejected this on the grounds that an exchange rate target could conflict with their goal of price stability. Some politicians have even proposed setting up a 'political counterweight' to the ECB.

Clearly, serious confrontations between the ECB and the politicians in the early years of EMU will make the Central Bank's life more difficult and any political tug-of-war could be further complicated by the regional structure of the ECB's executive board.

SUMMARY

Monetary policy is the cutting edge of economic and monetary union. As the EMU members are not in perfect economic synchronization, a single interest rate is bound to result in an uneven monetary 'pressure' being applied to different countries and individual governments will need to counteract any undue tightness or slackness through fiscal policy. The major challenge for the ECB will, however, be to convince the public that it has an accurate gauge for measuring price pressures – both inflationary and deflationary – across EMU as a whole and that its resulting monetary policy will foster an economic climate that encourages steady growth.

Chapter 12

FISCAL POLICY

Fiscal policy has not featured prominently in the theoretical consideration of optimum currency areas. This is logical in the sense that if a monetary union requires fiscal policy to make it work, it is clearly not an optimum area. Accordingly fiscal policy tended to be considered only in passing in the theoretical literature. Economic theorists simply acknowledged that in currency areas in which labour was immobile, an active fiscal policy would be necessary to reallocate demand from one region to another. In such cases it was asserted that fiscal policy ought to be centralized in order that this be carried out smoothly and efficiently (Kenen, 1969).

An EC Report in 1977, known as the MacDougall Report, considered in detail the role of fiscal policy in the Community. Here it was concluded that moves towards the stabilization of exchange rates, or monetary union, should involve a major centralization of European fiscal policies to the Commission, in order to cope with regional economic disturbances once currency adjustment was no longer available (European Commission, 1977). However, no moves were made down this route, which clearly implied some form of closer political integration.

The question of fiscal policy finally came to the fore in the 1989 Delors Report, which basically drew up the framework for EMU, that was incorporated in the Maastricht Treaty of 1992. Contrary to the MacDougall Report, the Delors Report acknowledged that Community-wide fiscal policy would remain relatively minor for the foreseeable future and that fiscal powers would still be the responsibility of the individual governments once EMU had taken place. However, the Report saw the need to provide some co-ordination of fiscal policies ahead of EMU, and this led to the Maastricht guidelines on budget deficits and debt. This in turn led to the proposed restriction on the size of individual countries' budget deficits after EMU (the 'stability pact').

In this chapter we will discuss, first, how fiscal policy ought in principle to work within a monetary union. Secondly, we will look at actual fiscal policy in the euro area and the implications of the stability pact.

FISCAL POLICY IN A MONETARY UNION

In terms of pure theory, the power of fiscal policy for an individual country should be greater under a fixed as opposed to a flexible exchange rate system (*see* Box 12.1). This implies that under EMU individual fiscal policies should have a crucial role to play in dealing with local economic fluctuations. But EMU members are likely to find that, in practice, fiscal policy is much less effective than the theory alone suggests. The main considerations are as follows:

Under EMU members are likely to find that fiscal policy is much less effective than the theory alone suggests.

1 Fiscal expansion cannot be financed by the creation of money, which under EMU is controlled by the European central bank; the degree of stimulus is thus much reduced. A country under EMU is effectively reduced to the status of a regional authority, albeit one with considerable tax-raising powers.

2 Individual EMU members are largely (to varying degrees) open economies, and openness is steadily rising as internal European trade increases. The more open an economy is, the more an

BOX 12.1

Economic theory: fiscal policy under fixed exchange rates

The relative merits of fiscal and monetary policy under alternative exchange rate regimes are normally assessed in terms of what is referred to as the 'Mundell–Fleming model'. This assumes a world of highly mobile international capital flows (as pertains today).

The reasoning of the Mundell–Fleming approach is as follows. An increase in fiscal spending promotes an increase in domestic demand. Under a flexible exchange rate system this results in higher interest rates, which in turn promotes a stronger currency. Both of these factors act to restrict the expansion of the economy – higher rates restrict domestic spending and the higher currency causes exports to fall. Thus the fiscal expansion is to a large extent self-defeating. By contrast an expansionary monetary policy immediately causes lower interest rates, as money supply is increased, and accordingly a lower currency. Thus monetary policy is doubly effective.

Under fixed exchange rates, by contrast, the reverse is true and monetary policy becomes ineffective. This happens because of the effect of highly mobile international capital flows. Any attempt to reduce domestic interest rates and expand money supply meets with a large capital outflow until interest rates are moved back up to previous (world-established) levels. As capital flows out, the central bank has to purchase domestic currency to maintain the fixed exchange rate, so that any money supply increase is reversed. If domestic interest rates cannot be changed, monetary policy clearly cannot have any effect. An increase in fiscal spending, by contrast, is effective because, unlike the case of floating rates, its impact cannot be offset by a rise in the exchange rate or in higher domestic interest rates.

This suggests that fiscal policy in a monetary union can operate as an effective stabilizer to deal with economic disturbances in member countries which no longer have their own monetary policy or exchange rate with which to operate.

increase in fiscal spending leaks away in the form of spending on 'imports' from elsewhere in the union.

3 Budget deficits financed by the issue of debt have their impact diluted to the extent that economic participants anticipate

higher taxes in the future to pay for them. Moreover, higher taxes, or the threat thereof, may lead to economic participants moving abroad, thus denuding the tax base.

4 A debt-financed budget deficit can only be continued for a certain period of time before the outstanding government debt builds up to levels that threaten to get out of control. In Italy, for example, gross debt as a proportion of GDP was only 58 per cent in 1980 but after several years of large deficits it had risen to over 100 per cent by 1991. Clearly, for a country which has a government debt of 100 per cent of GDP, most of its fiscal activity is engaged in servicing that debt. This means its freedom to engage in an active fiscal policy is much less than a country whose debt is only, say, 30 per cent of GDP.

Centralized fiscal policy

These arguments lead to the fundamental conclusion that, within a monetary union, fiscal policy is more effective if it is centralized. If Germany, for example, were to experience a boom and Spain a recession, higher tax receipts in Germany would automatically be transferred to pay increased unemployment benefit in Spain. The negative effects of an individual country having to smooth out its own economic cycles via a debt build-up do not arise.

A federal fiscal arrangment for a monetary union has an additional advantage. As well as short-term stabilization (i.e., over the duration of the economic cycle) a centralized entity can operate long-term fiscal transfers from richer to poorer regions within the whole of the union. This is a role that cannot be performed while regions effectively retain their own fiscal arrangements. The importance of this for a monetary union is that it can provide investment in poorer areas and thus promote convergence of productivity and economic efficiency across the union.

Within a monetary union, fiscal policy is more effective if centralized.

Such convergence is crucial in limiting the costs of the union and ensuring that it is successful.

Under EMU there is no prospect at present of a federal fiscal arrangement, since such a degree of political integration is not yet acceptable. The current EU budget amounts to only some 1 per cent of GDP, compared with national budgets of over 30 per cent, and thus is too miniscule to perform any stabilization role across countries.

The proposed fiscal set-up for EMU thus cannot be said to be optimal, although this does not necessarily mean that it is not workable. However, EMU fiscal policy is further complicated by the restrictions imposed on individual countries' budget deficits.

FISCAL POLICY UNDER EMU
The Maastricht criteria

The co-ordination of fiscal policies in the run-up to EMU was agreed in the Maastricht Treaty of 1992. The Treaty stipulated that, to be eligible for EMU, members should by 1997 have a budget deficit of 3 per cent or less of GDP and a gross national debt of 60 per cent or less of GDP. As we have have seen in the theoretical discussion of optimum currency areas, there is no reason why such rules should have been imposed on entry. More emphasis on convergence of economic cycles or labour markets would have been appropriate.

These minimum levels chosen for the Maastricht criteria thus had no particular economic significance, but were at least internally consistent. On the assumption that over the long term 5 per cent nominal GDP growth appears reasonable (which would comprise, say, 2.5 per cent real growth and 2.5 per cent inflation), then a budget deficit of 3 per cent, entirely financed by debt, would mean that a debt level of 60 per cent of GDP would remain stable indefinitely (i.e., $0.03 = 0.05 \times 0.6$).

These rules on debt and deficit reduction prior to EMU qualification were justified partly on the grounds of ensuring inflation convergence; clearly a country with a high government debt had the incentive to engineer a higher inflation rate in order to reduce the value of its debt. As it turned out, of course, inflation rates successfully converged in Europe while the debt ratios of several countries remained well above 60 per cent, but they were admitted anyway.

There was also a political dimension involved in the Maastricht rules. Germany hoped that by imposing strict fiscal discipline some of the less efficient economies, such as Italy, would be excluded from the EMU club, thus increasing the chances that the euro would become a hard currency. Ironically, all members achieved the 3 per cent budget deficit target for 1997, but not without some dubious accounting methods to which even Germany found it necessary to resort.

A more fundamental reason for restricting budget deficits appears to have been the question of solvency, i.e., ensuring that high debt EMU members are not under pressure to default by failing to service or repay their debt. As a rule, national governments with large deficits can always resort in the end to financing themselves by increasing the money supply, i.e., writing their own cheques to finance their spending. Since this is no longer feasible for EMU participants, there is a risk that a member country in fiscal difficulties may put pressure on the European Central Bank, or other members, to 'bail them out'. Accordingly, on the question of debt the Maastricht Treaty contained the following additional provisions:

1 The European central bank will not monetize (i.e., purchase) the debt of any issuing country
2 Neither the European Commission nor any member will be responsible for the debt of any other member.

The stability pact

Consideration was next given as to how fiscal policy should operate once EMU had begun. The fear emerged that once countries achieved the 3 per cent of GDP deficit required for entry (which only had to be achieved for the year 1997), their fiscal discipline would slip. Accordingly, some mechanism was required to ensure that discipline would be maintained under EMU. This resulted in the 'stability pact', agreed in 1996 at Amsterdam, which stipulated that budget deficits under EMU should in general remain 3 per cent or below. This clearly represented a major restriction on each country's fiscal policies. We need to consider how desirable this is and just how restrictive it will be.

Some mechanism was required to ensure that discipline would be maintained under EMU.

First, let us outline the provisions of the stability pact. These are somewhat convoluted, but may be summarized as follows:

1 If an annual budget deficit of 3 per cent or more is reported, the EU will request that it is corrected the following year.
2 If the offending country fails to correct the deficit, it will be obliged to lodge a non-interest-bearing deposit with the EU; if the deficit remains uncorrected, this deposit is converted into a fine two years later.
3 A country will not be obliged to take corrective action if the deficit is the result of severe recession, which is defined as a fall of 2 per cent or more in GDP the previous year.
4 In the event of a fall in GDP the previous year of between 0.75 per cent and 2 per cent, the offending country may make representation to the EU to the effect that the recession was none the less severe, in which case the authorities may deem that an excessive deficit may be acceptable without penalty.

Is the stability pact necessary?

Before considering the likely implications of these rules, it is interesting to consider whether or not such restrictions may actually be necessary.

The main reason for maintaining a deficit restriction under EMU appears to be that without it a member may borrow so much that it may be forced to default on its debt, which would thus undermine the credibility of the whole union. An additional reason is that some countries may borrow excessively on the EMU-wide capital market, and thus raise borrowing costs for other members. Such pressure on the EMU capital market may, it was feared, impose pressure on the European Central Bank to lower interest rates, and thus relax its monetary policy unnecessarily.

In our view, these fears are ill founded, for the following reasons:

1 Excessive borrowing by one member will not materially raise the overall level of market interest rates, which are determined by a whole variety of factors such as the level of economic activity and inflation. Instead, the effect would be to widen the spread the excessive borrower would pay over the market rate, thus discouraging its future borrowing (as, for example, happens for the Canadian provinces).

2 This being the case, there is no reason to expect the Central Bank to be unduly expansive in its policy; moreover, a properly independent Central Bank would in all likelihood be more restrictive than otherwise if it saw fiscal policies which were too loose on the part of some members.

3 Countries will be aware that the options to finance debt by creating money and inflating it away, or borrowing domestic currency and devaluing, no longer exist; they should therefore be more cautious in spending excessively.

4 In any event, the risk of a default by any EMU member may be

regarded as extremely low, given the extent of tax-raising powers.

It must also be pointed out that the explicit provisions of the Maastricht Treaty, namely that neither the Union, the Central Bank nor any other member are obliged to bail out a country spending excessively, should render the stability pact unnecessary. Indeed, the adoption of the stability pact itself probably undermines the 'no bail out' clauses to some extent, because the stated need for the pact appears to question their credibility.

However, the main disadavantage of the stability pact is that it hampers the operation of fiscal policy. It could do this in the following ways:

- By requiring that countries must stay within the 3 per cent limit it restricts the operation of 'automatic stabilizers', i.e., the lower taxes and higher government spending (such as unemployment benefit) that automatically occur during a downturn.
- Countries may feel obliged to run unnecessarily tight fiscal policies during an economic expansion in order to avoid coming up against the limit during the next downturn.
- By creating a bias towards unnecessarily tight fiscal policies, it risks throwing the burden of economic stabilization onto monetary policy, which may thus become more expansionary than otherwise; so, although designed to safeguard the autonomy of monetary policy, its effect might be just the opposite.
- Flexibility of fiscal policy is restricted just at the time when it is most needed, namely when European economies are adjusting to the implementation of EMU and the loss of independent monetary and exchange rate policy.

The stability pact in practice

Under the stability pact, the 3 per cent limit is waived in the event of a 2 per cent fall in GDP. This is likely to be invoked infrequently, since a fall in GDP of such magnitude in one year is highly unusual. But how restrictive is the 3 per cent limit itself? It is instructive to look at what would have happened if the pact had been in force over the last 30 years.

Table 12.1 summarizes trends in the budget deficits of EMU members over this period. It is clearly apparent that deficits have regularly been at or above the 3 per cent limit, which means that the scope for active fiscal policies would have been very much constrained had the pact been in force throughout this period.

Table 12.1 Average budget surplus (+) or deficit (–)

	1970–73	1974–85	1986–90	1991–95	1996–97	1998
Germany	0.2	–2.8	–1.5	–2.9	–3.1	–2.6
France	0.7	–1.7	–1.8	–4.5	–3.6	–2.9
Italy	–5.4	–9.6	–10.9	–9.2	–4.7	–2.6
Spain	0.4	–2.8	–4.0	–5.8	–3.7	–2.1
Netherlands	–0.5	–3.6	–5.1	–3.6	–1.6	–1.4
Belgium	–3.4	–7.8	–7.1	–5.8	–2.6	–1.3
Austria	1.5	–2.3	–3.2	–3.8	–2.8	–2.2
Finland	4.6	3.7	4.0	–5.3	–2.3	0.7
Portugal	1.9	–6.7	–4.5	–5.4	–2.9	–2.3
Ireland	–4.1	–10.4	–5.5	–2.2	0.3	2.1

% of GDP, yearly averages

Source: *European Economy, Supplement A No. 10*, October 1998

Economies only have to grow by less than capacity (which is about 2 per cent a year) for the automatic effects of lower taxes and higher spending to cause deficits to increase. For every 1 per cent below the level of full capacity in GDP per annum, budget deficits in EMU countries rise by around 0.5 per cent of GDP. So it does not necessarily take a recession to get deficits up to 3 per cent, just an extended period of slow growth. It is thus difficult to disagree with the OECD's conclusion that the 'practical implication of the pact is that, to give room for automatic stabilizers to work without hitting the 3 per cent limit, member states will need to continue fiscal consolidation for some time to come' (OECD, 1997).

The problem becomes more pressing when it is borne in mind that many countries have begun EMU at or close to the 3 per cent maximum. Their scope for discretionary fiscal policies is thus very limited.

A further question that has to be posed is how much notice will be taken of these regulations? It has been pointed out that the deficit curbing process involves somewhat long time lags (Artis and Winkler, 1997). Once an excessive annual deficit is identified (in March of the following year) a further seven months can elapse before corrective action has to be taken by the country concerned. The effects of this will not become measurable until March of the year after (i.e., two years after the first identification). If the corrective action taken is seen to be ineffective, only then is the offending country forced to make a deposit, which then becomes a fine a further two years later if the deficit is still uncorrected.

The system is clearly open to abuse in several ways:

- Countries may be tempted to 'fudge' budget forecasts; indeed, some of the measures taken to fulfil the Maastricht criteria for entry do not provide any optimism on this score.
- Countries may enact only token measures when required to take corrective action, in the hope that the deficit problem may have resolved itself by the time the following year's figures become available.
- There is nothing to stop countries violating the rule consistently provided that the deficit comes back down before a fine has to be paid.
- The regulation that the 3 per cent level 'may' be suspended if GDP falls by over 0.75 per cent is open to interpretation; the precise wording reads that when invoking this clause 'Member States will, as a rule, take as a reference point an annual fall in real GDP of at least 0.75 per cent'. The words 'may' and 'as a rule' seem to allow a good deal of leeway in interpretation.

It is possible, therefore, that the stability pact in practice will not be as restrictive as it appears. This does, however, mean that it runs the risk of bringing the worst of both worlds, namely hampering the implementation of fiscal policy without imposing any real control over it. Furthermore, since problems may arise early on, given the proximity of several members to the 3 per cent limit, it runs the risk of undermining the credibility of EMU at a crucial formative stage.

It is possible that the stability pact in practice will not be as restrictive as it appears.

FISCAL POLICY IN OTHER MONETARY UNIONS

It is interesting to compare the proposed fiscal arrangements of EMU with those of other existing large currency areas.

In the US, regional economic stabilization is carried out primarily at the Federal level. It has been estimated that something like a third of cyclical GDP downturns in US regions are cushioned by Federal taxes and transfers (Bayoumi and Masson, 1994), although some economists dispute the size of this cushioning effect and feel that it may be somewhat lower (Fatas, 1998). Federal flows also provide for sizeable long-term redistribution from richer areas to poorer areas. State governments in the US by contrast tend to run balanced budgets. This occurs primarily for historical reasons rather than by diktat from the Federal government (Eichengreen and von Hagan, 1995), but what is important is the fact that fiscal stabilization is essentially centralized.

A similar system prevails in Canada, although here the federation is somewhat looser than the US. Cyclical stabilization from the centre to the provinces is about half that of the US (Bayoumi and Masson, 1994) since individual provinces have more freedom than the US states to carry out their own fiscal policies. There are, however, much larger long-term redistributive flows conducted by the Federal government from rich to poor regions. Fiscal transfers appear to be particularly large in the case of the province of Alberta, which is oil dependent and whose prosperity swings with long-term fluctuations in the oil price.

Evidence from other federal countries indicates that such countries tend to have some degree of decentralized decision-making, but there is no consistent pattern of centrally imposed restrictions on their activity, on the lines of the stability pact (Eichengreen and von Hagan, 1995).

CONCLUSIONS

We have seen that the sort of fiscal arrangement proposed for EMU is not ideal in the sense that fiscal stabilization is more efficiently conducted from the centre. This also appears to be the case from observation of existing large federal currency unions such as the US and Canada.

It is certain that localized downturns will occur under EMU due to the lack of labour mobility, which will need a fiscal response to deal with them. Unfortunately, the implementation of local fiscal policies will be hampered by the provisions of the stability pact. Although countries may avoid following this pact to the letter, it is still likely to prove an unnecessary complication to an already difficult situation.

The fundamental question is: can EMU function efficiently with the proposed fiscal set-up? It may not necessarily be true that the US, for example, survives as a monetary union purely because of its centralized fiscal policy. The US was, after all, a monetary union for a considerable length of time before active fiscal management emerged *post* the Second World War. None the less, the troubling fact remains that Europe is burdened with considerably less flexible labour markets than the US or Canada, which in theory should require a more efficient fiscal arrangement to offset this, rather than the sub-optimal situation that exists.

It may well become apparent as EMU proceeds that a more centralized fiscal organization is required for EMU to survive, which will necessitate fundamental moves towards political integration. This is especially likely if the implementation of the stability pact turns out, as is quite probable, to be something of a mess. Thus it may be that EMU in the long run may move towards a similar framework to that of Canada, with a degree of local fiscal autonomy but a high degree of centralization.

Part

5

IMPLEMENTING EMU

Having considered the fundamental background factors, Part 5 will examine the practical problems involved in actually implementing EMU. Chapter 13 will consider the euro bloc as a whole in the context of the crucial economic factors outlined earlier, namely the labour market, trade structure, and economic convergence. We will extend this analysis in Chapter 14 by considering the EMU participants individually, and identifying the main problems faced by each. Lastly, in Chapter 15, we will apply this analysis to current EU members not participating in the first wave, and will consider when and if they are likely to join.

Chapter 13

THE EURO BLOC AS AN OPTIMUM CURRENCY AREA

The theory of optimum currency areas indicates that there are three main criteria for a successful currency union. These are:

- the mobility of labour,
- the degree of economic openness and the structure of trade, and
- the extent of convergence in economic activity.

How does the euro area itself stand with regard to these criteria?

LABOUR MARKET

A reasonably efficient labour market is crucial if monetary union is to succeed. Without the stimulation to the regional economies of the EMU area from currency adjustment, the unemployed have to move to where the jobs are. We will look at the European labour market in detail and compare it with the labour market in other existing (and successful) monetary unions, such as the US and Canada.

It is apparent from Table 13.1 that unemployment in Europe rose dramatically in the 1970s. Having averaged 2.5 per cent in the 1960s it has been at 9–10 per cent since 1980. Experience has varied across the EMU countries but all have been subject to the same broad trend and the spread between highest and lowest has widened. The recent European economic recovery has made no more than a minor dent in the overall long-term rise.

Table 13.1 Unemployment (%)

	1961–70	1971–80	1981–90	1991–94	1995–97	1998
Germany	0.7	2.2	6.0	5.4	9.0	9.7
France	1.8	4.1	9.2	11.0	12.2	11.7
Italy	4.8	6.1	8.8	9.9	12.0	12.0
Spain	2.5	5.4	18.5	20.5	22.0	18.9
Netherlands	0.9	4.4	8.5	6.3	6.1	3.7
Belgium	2.1	4.6	9.7	8.2	9.6	8.3
Austria	2.0	1.6	3.4	3.8	4.2	4.4
Finland	2.0	4.1	5.5	14.0	14.9	11.6
Portugal	2.5	5.1	7.0	5.2	7.1	5.7
Ireland	5.4	7.7	14.7	15.0	11.3	8.7
Average	2.5	4.5	9.1	9.9	10.8	9.5
Spread	4.7	6.1	15.1	16.7	17.8	15.2

Source: *European Economy No 64* 1997, *Supplement A No 3/4*, March–April 1998, and *Supplement A No 10*, October 1998

Further problems become apparent if we look at the labour market within each country. Table 13.2 shows the spread of unemployment across the regions of individual EMU members.

Table 13.2 Regional unemployment rates – April 1996 (%)

	Italy	France	Germany former West	Germany former East	Spain	Finland	Netherlands	Belgium	Austria	Portugal
low	5.3	9.6	5.3	11.7	17.9	12.7	5.8	7.1	3.8	4.1
:	5.3	10.7	5.5	15.1	19.4	15.8	5.9	12.9	4.7	7.0
:	6.3	10.7	6.4	15.3	20.4	16.1	6.2	14.1	5.5	8.9
	8.1	10.8	6.5	15.8	20.6	19.1	8.3			
	8.6	11.5	8.4	16.6	22.2	19.3				
	13.2	12.6	8.5	17.8	31.3					
:	20.2†	16.1								
	24.0†	16.8								
high	25.5†									

† southern regions

Major regions only included (in excess of 4 per cent of GDP)

No figures available for Ireland

Source: Eurostat, *Regions Yearbook 1997*

It is apparent that some countries suffer from woefully inefficient labour markets. Whereas a country such as the Netherlands has a very low spread of regional unemployment, from 5.8 per cent to 8.3 per cent, Italy and Spain have very wide regional disparities. The problem is particularly acute in Italy, where unemployment in the south is a staggering five times that of the most prosperous northern regions. Germany also has a major problem, resulting from its incomplete economic union with the former East. Whereas the regions of the former West are efficient, with a range of only 5.3 per cent to 8.5 per cent, unemployment in the East ranges up to 17.8 per cent. Other countries lie between these two extremes. But considering the small geographical size of some of these countries, the regional spread is still disturbingly wide. In a small place like Belgium, for example, it varies from 7.1 per cent to 14.1 per cent.

> *It is apparent that some countries suffer from woefully inefficient labour markets.*

Table 13.3 backs up these figures by comparing the spread of regional unemployment with annual interregional migration. There is a clear relationship between the two, with low migration tending to correspond with a high spread of regional unemployment, and vice versa. The point that clearly emerges is that in some countries labour simply does not move to eradicate local unemployment. The southern economies, Italy, Spain and Portugal, have by far the lowest rates of internal migration, and, in the cases of Spain and Italy, this is reflected in very high regional unemployment. Germany has a major adjustment problem with the assimilation of the East.

This is a snapshot of a particular year, but if we look back we see that the same regions continually experience higher unemployment. In Italy, for example, the south has consistently suffered. Indeed, the problem is getting worse – twenty years ago its unemployment was only twice that of the north.

Table 13.3 Regional unemployment and annual interregional migration

	Regional unemployment*	Interregional migration†
Netherlands	2.5	1.6
Belgium	7.0	1.3
Finland	6.6	1.3
Germany (West)	3.2	1.2
France	7.2	1.1
Spain	13.4	0.6
Italy	20.2	0.5
Portugal	4.8	0.3

* spread between highest and lowest

† % of total population

Figures not available for Austria and Ireland

Source: Eurostat, *Regions Yearbook 1997*

The worrying aspect of this is that, if labour markets are not efficient within some of these countries, we cannot expect them to
work efficiently across the whole EMU area, given the additional
cultural and language barriers involved.

The US – an efficient monetary union

How efficient does the labour market need to be for EMU to work?
It is useful to compare the European labour market with that of a
successful monetary union – namely, the United States. The US is
roughly the same size as the EMU bloc in terms of GDP, although
larger geographically. Regional trends in the 51 US states are summarized in Table 13.4 .

It is apparent that the spread has generally been lower than the
regional rates within most individual European countries. But compared with the spread across the European bloc as a whole, which
is the relevant comparison for the purposes of EMU, it is considerably lower. Unemployment across European countries in 1998 varied from 4 per cent to 19 per cent, and such a spread has prevailed
since the early 1980s. But in the US the spread has only varied

Table 13.4 Regional unemployment in the US

Unemployment range (%)	No of states in each range		
	1980	1990	1996
under 4%	–	4	7
4–5	6	13	15
5–6	9	22	18
6–7	11	9	6
7–8	16	2	3
8–9	5	1	2
9–10	3	–	–
over 10	1	–	–
total number	51	51	51
average rate for all US	7.1	5.6	5.4
lowest rate	4.0	2.2	2.9
highest rate	12.4	8.4	8.5
spread	8.4	6.2	5.6

Source: *1997 Statistical Abstract of the United States*, Department of Commerce

between 6 per cent and 8 per cent. Perhaps most importantly, states with high unemployment tend to move down after a few years, and vice versa. For example, in 1980 the state with the highest unemployment was Michigan with 12.4 per cent. By 1996 its unemployment was down to 4.9 per cent, comfortably below the average. Californian unemployment was 6.8 per cent in 1980, below average, but by 1996 was 7.2 per cent, one of the three highest.

Clearly this a flexible labour market. How much more flexible than Europe is apparent from the fact that interstate migration amounts to about 3 per cent of the total population per year (OECD, 1994). As comparison with Table 13.3 shows, this is about twice the rate of the Netherlands and three times that of France and Germany. For Italy and Spain the difference is even more marked.

What happens in the US is that labour is highly sensitive to local fluctuations in wage rates. Eichengreen (1993) has estimated that the response of labour to changes in wage rates in the US is five times higher than in the UK (which has one of the highest levels of labour mobility in Europe) and ten times higher than in Italy. It is clear that labour flows swiftly from state to state in the US to iron out localized fluctuations in economic activity. As we saw in Part 3, this is precisely what should happen in an optimum currency area.

Labour mobility across Europe

If labour markets within European country boundaries show relatively little mobility, to varying degrees, what about the extent of labour flows across national boundaries under EMU? The extent of these flows is apparent from the number of residents of each EMU country living in other EMU countries. This is illustrated in Table 13.5. The percentage of the total EMU population resident in another EMU country was only 1.2 per cent in 1995, identical to the figure in 1988. The figures are low across most of the bloc, with

Table 13.5 Labour movement across Europe

Country	Other EMU residents living in country*		Own residents living elsewhere in EMU*	
	1988	1995	1988	1995
Germany	1.2	1.6	0.2	0.3
France	2.7	2.2	0.4	0.5
Italy	0.1	0.2	2.0	1.9
Spain	0.3	0.4	1.4	1.1
Netherlands	0.8	0.9	1.4	1.5
Belgium	5.0	4.9	1.1	1.3
Austria	n/a	n/a	n/a	2.5
Finland	n/a	0.0	n/a	0.4
Portugal	0.2	0.3	9.2	9.0
Ireland	n/a	0.4	0.5	0.9
Total EMU	1.2†	1.2†	1.2†	1.2†

* % of each country's population
† % of total EMU population

Source: Eurostat, *Yearbooks*

few exceptions, although Belgium had a high percentage of residents from other countries (5 per cent), while a large percentage of Portuguese live outside the country (9 per cent), mostly in France.

Much of the movement tends to be only to neighbouring countries; for example, of the 2.5 per cent of Austrians living elsewhere in the area, 2.3 per cent were in Germany. As might be expected, there appears to be little in the way of labour flows to the southern countries, but some movement to the more prosperous northern countries, Belgium, Germany and France. Not suprisingly, there is little in the way of labour flows to and from Finland. Overall, the picture looks very static, with virtually no change between 1988 and 1995.

But just how low the movement is becomes apparent if we remember that these figures represent the total stock of immigrants over a period of many years, rather than an annual flow. Annual migratory flows were estimated by Eurostat for the year 1990, and are shown in Table 13.6. The figures are miniscule, with only 0.12 per cent of the population changing country during the year. To

Table 13.6 Annual migration in Europe, 1990

Country	From other EMU countries	Own residents to elsewhere in EMU
Germany	0.12	0.11
France	0.11	0.12
Italy	0.10	0.10
Spain	0.09	0.06
Netherlands	0.16	0.17
Belgium	0.35	0.31
Portugal	0.11	0.36
Ireland	0.16	0.27
Total EMU	0.12†	0.12†

% of each country's population
† % of total EMU population

Source: Eurostat, *Social Portrait of Europe*, 1995

put this in perspective, this 0.12 per cent compares with the 3 per cent of the population that change states every year in the US.

A revealing insight into Europe's labour market can be given by comparison with another existing monetary union, Canada. OECD figures show that an average of 1.5 per cent of Canadians change provinces every year. This is less than the US, but much higher than across Europe (OECD, 1994). However, Quebec is a major exception to the rest of Canada. Those living outside Quebec are six times more mobile from province to province than are inhabitants of French-speaking Quebec, who tend to remain within their own provincial border (McCallum, 1997). This undoubtedly reflects the importance of the language barrier in labour mobility, which helps explain the extremely limited mobility across national boundaries in Europe.

Reasons for labour market inflexibility in Europe

One of the main reasons for inflexibility in the European labour market is the extent of regulatory control. This is another marked difference between Europe and the US. The main effect of this is to seriously limit the efficiency of the market.

The most important regulations in Europe are as follows.

- Hiring and firing restraints. These include stipulations on the amount of severance pay, and notice of dismissal; such measures limit the extent of job creation and cause labour that might be more efficiently employed elsewhere to remain in unproductive jobs.
- Generous unemployment benefits. These promote higher long-term unemployment as recipients become reliant on them; long-term unemployment in the US as a proportion of the total is about one-third that of Europe; the long-term unemployed do not bother to look for jobs and become effectively cut off from the labour market.

- Statutory minimum wage. Relatively generous minimum wage rates in much of Europe promote higher unemployment in unskilled labour.
- Centralized wage bargaining. The tendency for wages to be fixed centrally in European countries means that jobs cannot be created in poorer areas where people might be prepared to work for less.
- Payroll taxes. European countries typically have high payroll taxes and other compulsory payments such as social security contributions; these are roughly three times higher than in the US per employee.
- Restrictions on hours worked per week, which discourage job creation in sectors in which flexibility of hours might be necessary.

These regulations all limit flows of labour in and out of employment and suppress the workings of the market mechanism. Moreover, if we look at how the Europe-wide labour market will have to work under EMU we have the additional problems of:

One of the main reasons for inflexibility in the European labour market is the extent of regulatory control.

- language and cultural barriers
- the fact that labour market regulations remain the province of each country and thus differ markedly from country to country; this confusion must limit labour's desire to move across national boundaries
- differences in equivalence of qualifications from country to country.

It is true that measures have been taken to try and improve the efficiency of Europe's labour markets. For example, the minimum wage for young people has been cut in Belgium, France and Spain. Labour market reforms in the Netherlands have gone a long way to reducing unemployment in that country by encouraging the use of part-time labour. However, most of these reforms are limited in scope and will do little to encourage the Europe-wide labour market.

Clearly it would be unrealistic to expect the European labour market to become like that of the US, which has a long tradition of high mobility originating from the pioneer days. Such an extent of free market economics in labour matters would be socially unacceptable by European standards. But in the context of EMU it is clear that much of Europe falls far short of the degree of labour mobility required for a monetary union.

OPENNESS AND TRADE STRUCTURE

The degree of trade openness is another important factor in considering which countries should participate in a monetary union. Basically, in open economies exchange rate adjustment is not a useful mechanism. Currency depreciation, for example, just causes inflation. But in closed economies the exchange rate is necessary to prevent competitiveness with the rest of the world being eroded by domestically generated inflation.

The relevant considerations regarding trade structure are the extent to which trade occurs with the other members of the union, and the impact it has on the economy. An open economy would not be suitable for monetary union if its trade is primarily with members outside the union. This data is summarizied in Table 13.7, which shows for each EMU member the proportion of trade with the rest of the EMU bloc (column b) and the proportion of trade outside the EMU bloc (column c). Both are expressed as a percentage of GDP so we can see the impact these trade flows have on each country's economic activity.

The first point to note about this table is that total trade of the EMU bloc with outsiders amounts to only 13.4 per cent of GDP.

Table 13.7 Trade as % of GDP*

	Total	With euro area	Outside euro area
	(a)	(b)	(c)
Germany	23.3	10.3	13.0
France	22.4	11.8	10.6
Italy	23.7	11.6	12.1
Spain	24.0	14.0	10.0
Netherlands	50.0	27.4	22.6
Belgium	65.0	41.6	23.4
Austria	38.8	24.4	14.4
Finland	33.5	11.2	22.3
Portugal	36.9	24.1	12.8
Ireland	74.0	23.5	50.5
Total euro area			13.4
United States			11.9

* Average of exports and imports of goods and services, 1995

Source: *OECD Economic Outlook*, December 1997

This is approximately the same figure as for US external trade. So after EMU these countries together represent a closed economy with the outside world, similar in nature to the US. Overall, therefore, the common currency is eminently feasible on this criterion: a collection of largely open economies become one closed economy under EMU.

If we look at the countries individually, however, we see that they are not all uniformly suitable. For most of the very open economies, namely Belgium, the Netherlands, Austria and Portugal, trade with the rest of the bloc is significantly larger than with outside countries, such that they may be expected to interlock well into the euro economy. The figures for Germany, France, Italy and Spain are somewhat less supportive, but acceptable. They are less open economies than the others and their trade with the rest of the bloc is of the same size as with outside members.

The problem countries are Ireland and Finland. In Ireland, largely because of its links with the UK, trade with outside areas constitutes 50 per cent of GDP and only 23.5 per cent occurs with its EMU partners. The Irish economy is thus likely to continue to be heavily influenced by outside factors, the most important of which is the UK economy. The same is true, to a lesser extent, of Finland, largely because of its trade links with Sweden.

ECONOMIC CONVERGENCE

Economic convergence refers to the extent to which the economies of Europe are becoming more similar and moving in unison. If the economies of the EMU bloc are converging, then there is less need for any exchange rate adjustment between them, since all economies will be in expansion or contraction together. There would also be less need for labour to flow from one country to another, since job markets would all be at a similar stage in the economic cycle. This is very important for EMU since it would mean that the inflexibility of the European labour market would be less of a disadvantage.

(1) Economic diversification

This convergence can be looked at firstly in terms of diversification. If all members have a similar spread of industries, any one country is not likely to suffer an economic slowdown on its own due to a downturn in one particular sector. On this criterion, all members are similar in their spread of industries with the exception of Finland, whose economy is significantly influenced by the forest products industry. No other members are exposed to this industry to such an extent. Wood and paper products amount to nearly 30 per cent of Finnish manufacturing output, compared with an average of only 4.5 per cent in the rest of the euro area.

This problem can be highlighted by referring again to the experience of Canada. As with forest products in Finland, the Canadian province of Alberta differs from the rest of the country in that it is oil dependent. The economy of Alberta goes up and down with fluctuations in the oil price. Because it is part of the Canadian monetary union, Alberta cannot devalue when its economy is depressed by falling oil prices, but its labour mobility is very high. Migration into Alberta from elsewhere in Canada during the years of a strong oil price (1974 to 1982) caused the population to rise by 14 per cent. During the subsequent depressed years (1983 to 1988) emigration to other provinces caused it to fall by 5 per cent (McCallum,1997). This is clearly a flexible labour market, and cannot be compared with the miniscule labour flows that currently occur between Finland and the rest of the euro bloc.

(2) Productivity

Another measure of convergence is the level of labour productivity. This is potentially very important under EMU because if some countries are unproductive, they will not be able to compete in the European market without a currency to devalue. This is particularly true if wage bargaining becomes centralized across Europe – so that low productivity areas have to pay the same wages as high productivity areas. Table 13.8 shows GDP per head (as a measure of labour productivity) for each country in total and for each of its regions.

For the countries as a whole, all fall within a broad range of 10 per cent of the European average, with the exceptions of Spain and Portugal, but in some cases this disguises a severe regional disparity. Spain and Portugal will experience competitiveness problems, particularly in their poorer regions but the same is true for Germany and Italy. Although their overall productivity is high, some regions are clearly less productive. Germany, of course, has the former East, which may be regarded as a special case and one that is an adjustment problem, albeit a rather extended one, rather than a permanent feature. In the case

If some countries are unproductive, they will not be able to compete in the European market without a currency to devalue.

Table 13.8 Regional GDP per head (100 = EU average)

	Germany	Italy	France	Spain	Finland	Netherlands	Austria	Belgium	Portugal
highest	149	131	166	97	118	111	124	182	96
region	128	126	105	91	86	102	112	114	62
:	125	120	101	88	80	98	88	91	49
	112	117	100	68	79	90			
	103	117	95	66	72				
	100	106	93	60					
	99*	71†	92						
	57*	69†	88						
	54*	69†							
:	53*								
lowest	52*								
region	52*								
country	—	—	—	—	—	—	—	—	—
average	108	102	110	78	91	103	112	113	69

Regional figures not available for Ireland

Major regions only are included (in excess of 4 per cent of GDP)

* regions of the former East Germany

† southern regions

Source: Eurostat, *Basic Statistics of the European Union*, 1996

of Italy, by contrast, the problem of the unproductive south is a long-term structural one. In a successful currency union, one would expect productivity to converge across the whole area over the long term. This has clearly not been the case for some of these countries.

(3) Common economic cycle

The third measure of convergence is in terms of the economic cycle. It has become apparent over the last 20 years that a specifically European economic cycle has developed. Countries which used to correlate more with the US economy now move in line with the European cycle, which basically means Germany. This is illustrated in Table 13.9.

In this table a figure approaching 1 represents a perfect correlation and a figure approaching zero means no correlation at all. The

Table 13.9 GDP growth correlations in the euro area

	1977–86	1987–92 (H1)	1992 (H2)–96
Germany	0.89	0.28	0.93
France	0.72	0.85	0.99
Italy	0.93	0.65	0.92
Spain	0.21	0.62	0.94
Netherlands	0.76	0.60	0.89
Belgium	0.51	0.92	0.97
Austria	0.65	0.71	0.85
Finland	0.17	0.68	0.88
Portugal	0.48	0.43	0.41
Ireland	0.30	0.65	0.76

Source: *OECD Economic Outlook*, December 1997

figure for Germany during the middle period is distorted downwards by the effect of unification with the East, which because of Germany's pre-eminence may also have depressed some of the other figures in that column. But the picture for most countries in EMU is clearly one of increasingly close movement. Germany of course shows a high correlation, other than for the unification period, because it dominates the whole region itself, which thereby follows the German cycle. For France, Italy, Austria, Belgium and the Netherlands, what was generally a moderately close correlation up to the mid-1980s developed into a close one of 0.85 or more by the mid-1990s. In the case of Spain, a very weak relationship in the first period has now developed into a very strong one, after its membership of the EU in 1986 and the growth of its trade links. The figure for Portugal has remained surprisingly low but, given the closer structure of Portugal's trade now with the rest of the area, and its small size, this figure ought to increase.

The analysis of trade flows showed that Finland and Ireland may experience problems because of trade links with non-EMU countries. The above table shows that Finland has actually moved from a negligible correlation with the euro area to a much closer one over the last few years. But this has only occurred because Sweden has moved closer to Europe over this period as well. This may not be a permanent feature since while Sweden remains outside EMU it is free to pursue its own economic policies, and thus draw Finland along with it on a different path.

In the case of Ireland, we see that its relationship with the European economy has increased but, as we would expect from having looked at its trade flows, it is still significantly influenced by outside factors, in particular the UK economic cycle. Indeed, the figure for Ireland in the final column would be much lower if the boom years of 1997–8 were included.

Chapter 14

COUNTRY-BY-COUNTRY ANALYSIS

GERMANY

The German economy is by far the largest in Europe and, as such, it will be the motor that drives EMU forward. Economies such as Belgium, the Netherlands and Austria are, essentially, economic satellites that will be carried along in its slipstream. The future performance of the Germany economy is therefore crucial to the well-being of the whole EMU project.

The post-war revival of the West German economy was so successful that it was dubbed the 'economic miracle'. A great deal of the credit for this 'miracle' must be given to the Bundesbank, whose prudent monetary policy not only helped to underpin economic growth but also kept the currency strong. By the 1980s the exuberant growth of the earlier years was beginning to flatten out but the economy was essentially very sound. Then on 29 November 1989 events took an unexpected turn that was to shake the well-ordered German economy to its roots. The dismantling of the Berlin Wall resulted in the unification of East and West Germany in October 1990.

In economic terms, this was a marriage of Beauty and the Beast. The West German government had the choice of either trying to assimilate the East German economy gradually over a period of years or opting for an immediate fusion with the concomitant social and economic disruptions that this would produce. They chose the latter course, largely because it was felt that a gradual transition would involve a huge programme of subsidies which would eventually lead to structural distortions. Unfortunately, the dislocative effects of the 'short sharp shock' strategy have proved to be far more severe than was originally envisaged. Unemployment in the eastern states (or *Länder*) rose sharply as the rapid increase in wage costs and the unity monetary conversion made output uncompetitive and left producers without a market for their products.

The Bundesbank, which had vigorously opposed the one-for-one currency union, watched with growing alarm as their pessimistic predictions proved correct. As a result of the huge injection of funds from the West, demand in the East rose dramatically. West German exports fell sharply as producers tried to meet this surge in demand, turning the current account from a surplus to a deficit. The West German economy was already in a cyclical upswing and the additional demand began to push against capacity constraints. Inflation began to pick up sharply, rising to 4 per cent – an unacceptably high level by German standards. This, in turn, put upward pressure on wage settlements. The Bundesbank acted quickly to take the heat out of the economy. Monetary policy was tightened in 1991 and kept tight throughout the following year.

Germany had received an 'asymmetrical' shock that was to have severe repercussions on the other European economies that were tied into the Exchange Rate Mechanism. As these countries were committed to an exchange rate parity in which the Deutschmark was the anchor currency, they were obliged to raise their interest rates or risk their currencies coming under pressure. European interest rates therefore followed Germany's higher, tilting these economies into recession.

The scars etched on the national German psyche as a result of the inflationary excesses of the Weimar republic have meant that, over the years, German governments have tended to run a prudent fiscal policy but the costs of financing unification have wreaked havoc with the country's finances. The original cost projections were far too low as it was not appreciated that, at the time of unification, the East German economy was quite literally on the verge of collapse.

It has been estimated that, since 1991, the costs of unification have amounted to DM 140,000 million per annum and this is reflected in the budget figures.[1] From 1986–90, the average annual budget deficit was 1.5 per cent, whereas between 1991–5 it almost doubled to 2.9 per cent. Against this background of escalating costs, meeting the Maastricht debt criteria became an uphill task. By 1996, the budget deficit had risen to 3.4 per cent and as late as mid-1997 it was feared that, despite a package of measures designed to cut government spending by DM 40,000 million, the outturn for the year would be 3.5 per cent. Like some of his European counterparts, the finance minister Theo Waigel desperately sought some creative solution to avoid the ignominy that Germany might not qualify for EMU. However, his proposal of simply revaluing Germany's gold reserves received short shrift from the Bundesbank. Eventually two supplementary budgets and a spending freeze brought the budget deficit down to the 3 per cent target.

The high costs of unification have also resulted in a sharp rise in the level of gross debt as a percentage of GDP. In 1991, the figure was 41.5 per cent but by 1997 it had climbed to 61.3 per cent, just over the Maastricht limit of 60 per cent.

As discussed above, the process of unification has led to a dramatic deterioration in the level of employment in the eastern *Länder* of Germany but the western *Länder* have not been immune from problems. Germany's welfare provisions are very generous and consequently employers face high non-wage costs. In the early 1990s, German labour costs were the highest of all the major

[1] *Country Profile 1997–98*, page 21, The Economist Intelligence Unit

industrialized countries. Not surprisingly, German manufacturers began to relocate to other countries and the combination of this industrial exodus, coupled with falling demand as a result of the Bundesbank's monetary tightening, led to a steady rise in unemployment. In the last quarter of 1997, it reached a post-war peak of 11.8 per cent.

In terms of economic activity, Germany is ideally suited to being at the epicentre of EMU. The economy has always had a strong European focus with over 40 per cent of its foreign trade being carried out with other EU countries. The timing of the launch of EMU was, however, a little unfortunate coming as it did so soon after the re-unification. The social and economic repercussions of this massive operation are still being felt throughout the economy. In order to meet the challenges imposed by EMU, there will have to be further structural changes – the most important of which is the deregulation of the labour market and the reduction of non-wage costs. After a turbulent decade, Germany, therefore, must face a further testing period of change.

> *In terms of economic activity, Germany is ideally suited to being at the epicentre of EMU.*

FRANCE

As one of the two main axis countries propelling EMU forward, the performance of the French economy is of paramount importance in determining whether the next phase of European integration is a success or not. To a large extent, however, the formal adoption of economic and monetary union is, for the French, just a continuation of the *status quo*.

The French franc participated in the original currency 'snake' and was a founder member of the Exchange Rate Mechanism in

1979. But in the early years of European exchange rate manage-ment, the franc fell firmly into the 'weak currency' category and was forced to devalue on a number of occasions. In 1983, François Mitterrand, the socialist President, made an abrupt U-turn on eco-nomic policy. He re-introduced some of the economic measures that prime minister Raymond Barre had implemented in the 1970s to try and effect a radical restructuring of the ailing French econ-omy. Maintaining the value of the franc became a top economic priority, and this *franc fort* policy has – more or less – been adhered to over the past 15 years. It has not always been an easy policy to pursue. In 1983, to underline its commitment to this exchange rate policy, the Banque de France had to keep short-term interest rates six percentage points above German rates but gradually, over the years, growing credibility has enabled the differential to be whit-tled down (*see* Fig. 14.1).

The *franc fort* policy has been notably successful in wringing inflation out of the French economy. From having one of the highest inflation rates out of the original six EEC countries, France now boasts one of the lowest. Significantly, since 1990 French inflation has remained below that of Germany. There has, there-fore, been a considerable gain on the inflation front in maintain-ing a close link with the Deutschmark but this gain has been achieved at the expense of a high cost in terms of unemployment (*see* Fig. 14.2).

The high level of real interest rates, necessary to persuade the markets that the government was committed to using the exchange rate as a firm anchor for its monetary policy, has acted as a severe drag on the econ-

The franc fort *policy has been notably successful in wringing inflation out of the French economy.*

omy. Since 1986, the average annual rate of growth of real GDP in France has been 2.2 per cent – below the EMU members' average of 2.4 per cent over the same period. This below-trend growth,

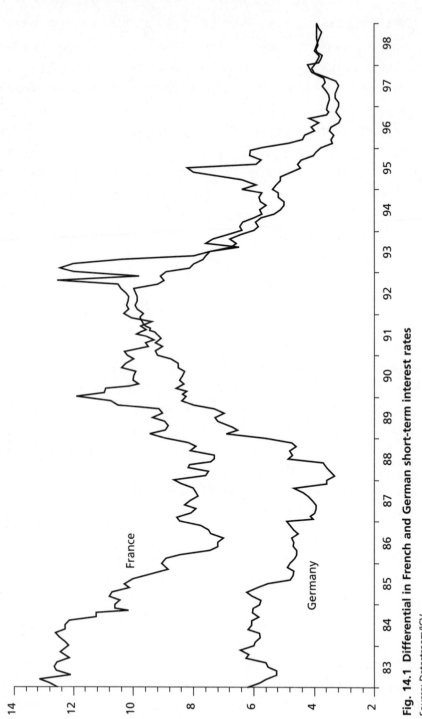

Fig. 14.1 Differential in French and German short-term interest rates

Source: Datastream/ICV

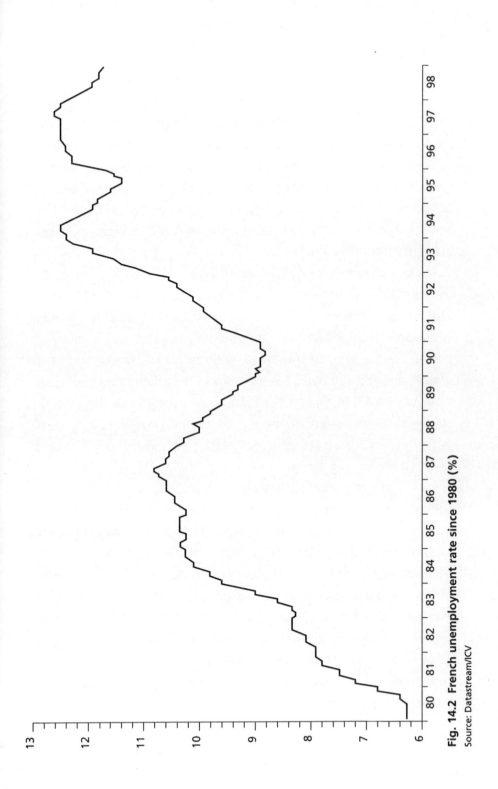

Fig. 14.2 French unemployment rate since 1980 (%)
Source: Datastream/ICV

combined with structural rigidities in the labour market, has resulted in high levels of unemployment. The major question for France is what proportion of this unemployment is due to the 'transitional' costs incurred while the economy has been adjusting to a regime of a fixed exchange rate and what proportion is due to structural inflexibilities in the labour market. A number of factors, such as regional disparities in unemployment, a mismatch between job skills and employment opportunities and the high cost to employers of increasing their work force, suggest considerable structural problems.

The traded goods sector accounts for just less than 25 per cent of overall GDP but, within this sector, half the activity is with other EMU participants and there will therefore be considerable benefits from lower transaction costs and greater price certainty. Germany is France's single most important trading partner, accounting for almost one-sixth of overall foreign trade, and there has been a significant pick-up in trade with Spain and Portugal since these countries became members of the EU. Moderate wage rises in recent years have increased France's competitive position, giving a strong boost to the export sector.

The high percentage of EMU-related trade flows, together with the exchange rate linkage, has helped to ensure that the economic cycle in France has, since the early 1990s, moved in almost perfect synchronization with that of the rest of Western Europe.

On the financial front, the economic slow-down in the early 1990s led to a sharp rise in the budget deficit and the government had great difficulty in bringing it down to meet the Maastricht criterion. Attempts by Prime Minister Juppé to rein back spending in 1995 were met with fierce public resistance. Despite this opposition some retrenchment was achieved and this, together with a pick-up in economic activity, helped to boost revenues but it was only by dint of some adroit fiscal manoeuvring over the partial privatization of France Télécom that the 1997 figure was squeezed down to the 3 per cent limit. The 1998 deficit of 2.9 per cent of GDP is the highest in the eurozone and allows little leeway for any economic downturn – especially if the government carries out its promise to relax fiscal policy.

By harnessing the franc to the Deutschmark for the past 15 years, the French economy has already made many of the adjustments necessary for a successful currency union. The most serious outstanding area of concern regarding France's participation in EMU is the level of structural unemployment. There needs to be a radical overhaul of French labour laws in order to promote greater flexibility but recent legislation has, in fact, been in the opposite direction and it is, therefore, questionable whether there is the political will to implement the necessary changes. Furthermore, unemployment is a politically charged issue and, if EMU is perceived to be aggravating the situation, there could be increased public resentment to France's participation. The risks surrounding France's membership of EMU are therefore more political than economic.

ITALY

Italy is third largest of the EMU economies, and more than twice the size of the next largest (Spain). This means that its ability to fit in comfortably could be crucial to the whole EMU venture.

In some ways Italy is an ideal candidate for the currency union. Its economic growth has followed a similar pattern to that of its EMU partners over a long period. With respect to trade flows Italy also interlocks well. Since joining the EEC as a founder member in 1957, trade with other members has increased substantially, such that nearly half of imports and exports are now with the euro bloc (the figure was only 25 per cent in 1958).

In terms of inflation Italy has achieved a remarkable reduction, bearing in mind that it peaked at over 20 per cent at one point in the 1970s and averaged 6 per cent in the early 1990s. The problem is that real convergence with the low inflation economies of Europe has been only a very recent phenomenon, and a longer track record of low inflation would have made us more confident that Italy can survive under EMU. As late as 1996 Italian inflation was still at 4.3 per cent, well above the European norm, so that it only really converged in the final two years before EMU began.

This poor inflation record made the Italian lira the weakest currency in the ERM. Between joining the system at its inception in 1979 and being forced out during the 1992 crisis, the lira was devalued 10 times. Against the Deutschmark this translated into a cumulative depreciation of 56 per cent over that period. The lira declined further after leaving the ERM, before the implementation of a series of tight economic policies during the mid-1990s helped to bring some recovery. The lira rejoined the ERM in 1996, but with a parity in Deutschmark terms still 24 per cent below the one at which it had left four years earlier.

The change in economic policy represented a desperate last ditch effort not to be left behind outside EMU. There has been a strong self-fulfilling element in this since, by becoming a serious candidate for EMU, Italy immediately inherited the low inflation credibility of the Bundesbank, with a consequent dampening effect on inflationary expectations. The problem is that this can just as easily be unwound if Italy is seen to be uncompetitive within EMU. Without a devaluation of the lira to bail the economy out, the tendency for domestic Italian inflation may reappear in the form of poor competitiveness and local recession.

Fiscal control had collapsed in Italy during the 1980s resulting in budget deficits averaging 11 per cent of GDP during the 1986–90 period and remaining over 9 per cent during the first half of the 1990s. This caused public sector debt to rise from an acceptable 58 per cent of GDP in 1980 to an alarming 125 per cent by 1994. Since a large proportion of government spending in Italy related to the huge costs of servicing the existing debt, the prospect of Italian EMU membership had a self-fulfilling effect similar to that on inflation. Lower inflationary expectations fed into lower interest rates, thus bringing spending on debt service down. Even so, Italy still only managed to get its deficit within the 3 per cent Maastricht limit in 1997 by means of the notorious fudge of the 'Eurotax' implemented in 1996. This was a temporary tax on incomes, to be repaid in 1999, and was really borrowing rather than actual deficit reduction. Thus the Italian government finances remain somewhat fragile and government debt is still over 100 per cent of GDP.

This brings us to the problem of the vast regional disparities. Whereas the north is industrialized, fully employed and prosperous, the south suffers from high structural unemployment and poverty. Labour fails to move from south to north to remove the differential, as it would in a flexible labour market. Labour productivity in the south is about 60 per cent that of the north.

If we could split Italy in two, we would find that the north would fit quite easily into EMU. But the south clearly does not.

Despite policies in place for some 30 years to resolve this problem, the north–south divide is as firmly entrenched as ever.

If we could split Italy in two, we would find that the north would fit quite easily into EMU. But the south clearly does not, and ideally should have its own currency to devalue in order to stimulate its competitiveness. The inescapable conclusion is that, a century and a quarter after political unification, Italy itself cannot be described as anything approaching an optimum currency area. Thus by joining an even larger currency area, there is a risk that regional difficulties may only get worse. This could in turn feed back into a deteriorating fiscal situation which the volatile world of Italian politics may not be able to control.

SPAIN

After joining the EC in 1986, the Spanish economic cycle began to move closely in phase with that of the rest of Europe. This has been reflected in the changing composition of Spain's trade. Trade with other members of the EMU area now stands at a high level of 58 per cent of the total, compared with 47 per cent ten years ago. In 1958 the figure was only 25 per cent. From this viewpoint, therefore, Spain fits very well into the euro economy, although 1997 and 1998 saw GDP growth accelerating significantly above the euro average.

Regarding inflation, the performance has been very much like that of Italy, with levels of 15–20 per cent in the 1970s giving way to around 6 per cent by the early 1990s. As with Italy, true convergence with the European norm only occurred in 1997 and 1998, so that it is not yet clear whether or not this performance is sustainable.

The government accounts remained relatively well controlled until heavy spending in the 1980s saw the budget deficit rise to a high of 7 per cent of GDP in 1985. Since then it has been a struggle to keep the deficit at manageable levels, and the 3 per cent Maastricht maximum was only obtained with some dubious accounting. On the positive side, however, the earlier period of fiscal control meant that Spain has not been burdened with the very high government debt levels experienced elsewhere. Gross debt was still only at 17.5 per cent of GDP in 1980, and despite rising significantly since then was still at a relatively manageable 67 per cent by 1998.

Spain has not been burdened with the very high government debt levels experienced elsewhere.

The Spanish peseta joined the Exchange Rate Mechanism in 1989 but was obliged to devalue three times during the 1992–93 exchange rate crisis, by a total of 19 per cent. It devalued a further

7 per cent in 1995, but subsequently maintained its parity up to the start of EMU. As with the Italian lira, it was a traditionally weak currency with only a limited recent period of stability.

The main problem with Spain is its labour market. It currently has the highest unemployment rate in the EU, and rather worryingly has maintained this undesirable position for most of the last 20 years. The problem really emerged following the implementation of labour market regulations in the early 1980s. Having been no higher than 5 per cent until 1977, unemployment rose to a high of over 21 per cent in 1986, before falling during the next expansion to 16 per cent in 1990. Following the slowdown in the early 1990s it rose again to 24 per cent in 1994. By 1998, despite four years of reasonably solid economic growth, it had only fallen to around 19 per cent. Thus the unemployment rate appears to ratchet higher with each succeeding economic cycle.

Unemployment is also a regional problem. It is very high in the poverty-stricken south, at over 31 per cent, and in the other five regions varies between 18 per cent and 22 per cent. The main explanation lies in the fact that, even by EU standards, the Spanish labour market is subject to excessive regulation. These include heavy taxes on employment, high costs of firing, and substantial unemployment benefits. Attempts have been made to bring reforms to the labour market, such as the introduction in 1997 of a more flexible work contract, but these are only at an early stage.

It is difficult to be optimistic as to how the Spanish labour market will fare under EMU. Certainly it would have been preferable to have seen some success from labour market reforms before joining the euro area, and high unemployment looks set to remain without the availability of the peseta to stimulate the local economy.

THE NETHERLANDS

Germany is by far the single most important trading partner for the Netherlands and, as part of the inner Deutschmark bloc, it is an obvious candidate for EMU.

The Dutch government has long recognized the significance of the country's trading relationship with Germany and, for this reason, the guilder joined first the 'snake' and then the Exchange Rate Mechanism. In the early 1980s the markets were sceptical about the guilder's ability to maintain a level pegging with the Deutschmark. Fiscal profligacy together with the oil crisis had, in the late 1970s, created serious economic problems but, for a while, these problems were camouflaged by the discovery of natural gas. In 1983 the then Prime Minister, Ruud Lubbers, decided that there needed to be a radical change in the country's economic programme in order to tackle what had come to be known as the 'Dutch disease'. He reined back fiscal spending and started to address some of the country's structural problems. The measures taken by his coalition government convinced the foreign exchange market that the economy was set on a more positive course and since 1983 the guilder has maintained its parity against the Deutschmark.

In 1996, the Netherlands had an annual GDP of $396bn, making it the fifth largest economy participating in EMU. Half of the country's economic activity is orientated towards the traded goods sector and 50 per cent of this overseas trade is with other EMU countries. In terms of trade flows, therefore, the Netherlands should fit very well into the European currency area.

Given such a heavy economic reliance on the rest of Europe, it is not surprising that the Dutch economic cycle has come to show an increasingly close correlation with that of its EMU partners. In the mid-1980s inflation dropped sharply and for the five years from 1986–90 the average annual rate was 0.9 per cent – the lowest in

Europe. It picked up again during the 1991–5 period as a result of the post-unification boom in Germany but this upsurge was checked by the monetary squeeze instigated by the Bundesbank.

The Dutch have made a start on deregulating their labour market and this has had a beneficial impact on the unemployment rate, which has been on a declining trend since the early 1990s. In 1998 Dutch unemployment was 3.7 per cent – the lowest in the EMU bloc. There has been some criticism that the high number of part-time workers in the Netherlands disguises the true rate of unemployment and, while there is no doubt some truth in this, it does nevertheless underline the flexible structure of the labour market.

As the Dutch began to take steps towards putting their public finances in order back in the 1980s, they have not had the same difficulty in meeting the Maastricht criterion with respect to the level of the public sector deficit as other EMU participants. The public sector deficit has been comfortably below the 3 per cent ceiling since 1996. The Dutch social security system is, however, still one of the most generous in Europe and there is therefore a risk that, if this is not trimmed back, the deficit could balloon rapidly above 3 per cent of GDP during a cyclical downturn. At 71.4 per cent, the gross debt to GDP ratio was above the Maastricht target of 60 per cent in 1997 but it is on a declining trend and is unlikely to pose any serious financial problems.

Since the mid-1980s, the Dutch economy has undergone an impressive transformation.

Since the mid-1980s, the Dutch economy has undergone an impressive transformation. From being synonymous with economic mismanagement, the 'Dutch model' now exemplifies sound financial practice and it is well placed both to meet the challenges of and to benefit from the trading opportunities that EMU will bring.

BELGIUM

Belgium has always been at the forefront of attempts to forge a closer European integration and, even before the launch of EMU in January 1999 it already had some experience of monetary union, having operated one with Luxembourg since 1935. (For the purposes of this analysis, the Belgium–Luxembourg Economic Union is considered as one economic entity that, with apologies to the Luxembourgers, is referred to as Belgium.)

In theoretical terms, Belgium's small, open economy makes it a classic candidate for EMU. Sixty-five per cent of the country's economic activity is geared towards foreign trade and 60 per cent of this trade is with the eurozone, so Belgium is well placed to take advantage of the benefits accruing from the formation of a single currency area. Its principal trading partners are Germany, the Netherlands and France, making it an integral part of the Deutschmark bloc. Interestingly, the proportion of foreign trade being carried out with Germany and the Netherlands has fallen slightly over the past decade as Belgium has expanded its trade links with some of the newer EU recruits.

Belgium's growth mirrors very closely that of the rest of Europe.

As a result of its high dependence on EU trade, Belgium's growth mirrors very closely that of the rest of Europe. Table 13.9 (*see* page 137) shows that during the period 1992–6 the correlation of Belgium's annual GDP growth with other EMU countries was an almost perfect 0.97, thereby very fully satisfying the convergence criterion.

Unfortunately, Belgium's economic performance has not always matched up to that of the rest of the Deutschmark bloc. From the mid-1970s to mid-1980s inflation in Belgium was significantly higher than that in either Germany or the Netherlands. This, in turn, put pressure on the exchange rate, which, in the early years of the ERM, was frequently the target of speculative selling. However, this pressure gradually abated as the inflation rate was brought down to German levels and since 1987 the Belgian franc has maintained its parity with the Deutschmark.

The main impediment to Belgium meeting the Maastricht criteria for qualification for EMU was the country's high level of debt. This built up rapidly in the 1970s and 80s as successive coalition governments lacked the political muscle to take the unpopular measures necessary to curb the deficit. In 1992 Prime Minister Dehaene obtained cross-party support for a major fiscal 'Consolidation Plan', designed to bring the economy into line with the Maastricht targets. The combination of tight fiscal restraint and a drop in interest rates brought the gross government debt down from a peak of 136.8 per cent in 1993 to 121.9 per cent in 1997. Although this was over double the Maastricht level of 60 per cent, it was deemed to be improving at a sufficiently 'satisfactory pace' (the let-out clause written into the Maastricht Treaty) to enable Belgium to qualify for EMU. The budget deficit has also dropped from an average of 5.8 per cent of GDP over the period 1991–5 to 2.0 per cent in 1997.

As far as the basic tenets of optimum currency theory are concerned, the real concern about Belgium is the level of unemployment stemming from structural rigidities in the labour market and the high non-wage costs. An unfortunate feature of this relatively small country is the regional disparity in levels of unemployment which can, to a large extent, be explained by the linguistic barrier between the Dutch-speaking Flemings who live in Flanders and the French-speaking people of Wallonia and Brussels.

Given its trade structure, the Belgian economy will undoubtedly benefit from the cost savings that monetary union with its main trading partners will bring. However, to capitalize fully on these opportunities, non-wage labour costs need to be reduced in order to improve Belgium's competitive position *vis-à-vis* its EMU partners.

AUSTRIA

Like a pawn on a chessboard, Austria was caught between the conflicting pulls of East and West during the Cold War years. In exchange for recognition of its sovereign status, Austria signed a treaty in 1955 agreeing to remain politically neutral. This meant that, although the country's trading focus was predominantly with the West, it could not be reinforced with closer political ties by, for example, joining the EEC. This political stalemate ended abruptly in the 1990s with the disintegration of the Soviet Union and in 1995 Austria joined the EU.

With foreign trade amounting to just under 40 per cent of GDP, the Austrian economy is an open economy and should, according to the precepts of optimum currency area theory, benefit from participation in a monetary union.

Trade with Germany is a very dominant feature of the Austrian economy, since it is more than four times larger than that of the next largest trading partner, Italy. With such a high proportion of trade either coming from or destined for Germany, Austria can be considered a German satellite economy and since the 1970s the Austrian schilling has been closely tied to the Deutschmark. This exchange rate policy has ensured that Austria has maintained a consistently good inflation performance relative to the other European countries.

The growing economic and political proximity to the other EMU economies is reflected in a closer correlation between the Austrian economic cycle and that experienced in the rest of the eurozone. But, in the years immediately following Austria's accession to the EU, the economy has had to grapple simultaneously with a number of different problems which have resulted in lower than average growth.

Membership of the EU brought increased domestic competition while, at the same time, the Maastricht straitjacket necessitated a tough fiscal programme. The collapse of communism has also given rise to greater entrepreneurial competition from Austria's eastern neighbours. Lastly, one of the country's main industries – tourism – has declined dramatically due to the high value of the Austrian schilling and the falling cost of long-distance exotic locations.

Austria has consistently boasted one of the lowest unemployment rates in Europe but this is, to some extent, a reflection of the relatively low retirement age and the large number of workers employed in the public sector. Both trends are likely to store up future fiscal problems.

The combination of privatization proceeds and a tight fiscal policy succeeded in bringing the fiscal budget down to 1.9 per cent of GDP in 1997 while the level of government debt stood at 64.3 per cent.

Austria has consistently boasted one of the lowest unemployment rates in Europe.

Austria therefore embarks on EMU in a relatively strong position but, like the other Deutschmark satellite countries, it will have to make changes in its social security provisions if it is not to risk losing ground to cheaper competition from both within the EU and eastern Europe.

FINLAND

Finland is one of the more unlikely members of EMU. It is the only Nordic country to participate, since Sweden and Denmark have both opted to stay on the sidelines for the time being. Finland is thus geographically and culturally remote from the rest of the EMU, lodged as it is between its two much larger neighbours Russia and Sweden.

During the Cold War Finland was in a somewhat precarious position. It was very much part of the West in terms of being a free market economy. But Finland was always conscious of its long border with the Soviet Union, which was also a major trading partner, and was careful to be seen as politically neutral. The collapse of the Soviet Union in the early 1990s provided Finland with the opportunity to embrace the West more closely and it thus enthusiastically joined the EU in 1995. Membership of EMU is an extension of this desire to be accepted as a fully fledged member of Western Europe.

However, its economic cycle has traditionally been dominated by events in Sweden (which enjoys a GDP twice that of Finland) and in Russia. In the early 1990s, Finland was knocked from both sides – first, by a recession in Sweden and, secondly, by the collapse of the Soviet Union. Finnish GDP actually fell for three years in a row from 1991 to 1993. In reaction to the severity of this downturn, the economy subsequently grew at around 5 per cent *per annum* for the next four years. So its economy cannot at present be said to be in phase with those of its EMU partners. Indeed Finnish GDP growth correlates much more closely with that of Sweden than that of Germany.

The structure of trade has in recent years moved towards the EMU bloc. Trade with Sweden remains important and currently stands at approximately 11 per cent of Finland's total, although the proportion is falling, having been over 14 per cent ten years ago. At the same time trade with its EMU partners has risen to 32 per cent of total exports and imports. This is still relatively low, however, compared with other EMU members.

> *The structure of trade has in recent years moved towards the EMU bloc.*

It would clearly be helpful if Sweden were to participate in the euro, thus reducing Finland's exposure to fluctuations in the Swedish krona. This is particularly a problem in the pulp and paper industry, which, although not quite as totally dominant in the economy as in the past, is still extremely important and accounts for one third of exports. EMU creates a problem, first, because these products are priced in US dollars and, secondly, competitors in the equivalent sector in Sweden have the potential advantage of a weaker Swedish krona. It is thus not suprising that the Finnish pulp and paper industry has been very much against membership of EMU.

The Finnish markka remained outside the ERM until October 1996. Before that it was managed against a trade-weighted basket and was normally adjusted by the Central Bank in line with the Swedish krona to ensure competitiveness. By being in the ERM, while Sweden remained outside, Finland began to assert its financial independence from its neighbour. But whether or not this is viable over the long term remains to be seen.

In common with other countries, Finland experienced very high inflation in the 1970s (it peaked at nearly 20 per cent in 1974). More recently, the recession in the early 1990s had a major beneficial impact. Inflation fell from 6.0 per cent in 1990 to only 0.3 per cent in 1995 and remained low in subsequent years.

Regarding the government accounts, Finland had for many years run a budget surplus, until the last recession caused an abrupt move into deficit, which reached a peak of 8.0 per cent of GDP in 1993. The strong economic recovery after 1994 brought this back into balance, so that Finland comfortably met the 3 per cent Maastricht guideline. The recession also caused a sharp rise in government debt in the 1990s, but it remained under the 60 per cent of GDP limit.

Unemployment, although down from the highest level of over 17 per cent seen during the recession, has remained high and was still at 12 per cent in 1998. Moreover, labour mobility with the rest of Europe is virtually negligible. How well the labour force will mesh with that of the EMU bloc, given Finland's remoteness, is a major concern.

In summary, Finnish membership of EMU has been primarily

politically driven and problems exist on the economic side. These are the structure of trade and the recent roller-coaster nature of its economic cycle. Swedish membership of EMU would go a long way to resolving these problems but this remains a major uncertainty.

PORTUGAL

A few years ago the idea that Portugal would participate in EMU at the outset would have been considered extremely fanciful. As recently as 1991 the inflation rate was 12.2 per cent, which was about twice as high as even Spain and Italy were recording at that time. However, in the course of the 1990s a determined sequence of austerity measures, accompanied by large-scale privatization of national industries, brought inflation under control and restored the viability of the private sector.

Portugal is the second smallest of the EMU participants (ranking above Ireland). It is less than 5 per cent of the size of the German economy and 18 per cent of the size of its immediate neighbour Spain. Until Portugal joined the EC along with Spain in 1986, political and economic relations between the two neighbours were circumspect. Since then much has changed and Portugal is no longer a remote corner of Europe.

A major positive factor for Portugal is that its trade with the EMU bloc now accounts for a very high 66 per cent of its total.

A major positive factor for Portugal is that its trade with the EMU bloc now accounts for a very high 66 per cent of its total. Despite this, Portuguese GDP growth has not correlated well with that of the rest of Europe, and has exhibited large and volatile fluctuations. The 1996–98 period saw GDP growing at around 4 per cent *per annum* and, unlike the bulk of the euro area, approaching the top of its economic cycle just at the start of EMU.

However, since the economy is quite open, with the external

sector representing 37 per cent of GDP, the extent of trade with the EMU area ought to encourage economic activity to move more in line with the rest of the area than it has done until now.

As a result of the fiscal measures noted above, the budget deficit came down rapidly in the 1990s and Portugal came in under the 3 per cent Maastricht limit relatively comfortably in 1997. This also brought inflation down sharply over the same period, such that by 1997 it was only 2.5 per cent. However, the rapid economic activity caused the rate to move up slightly in the course of 1998.

The Portuguese escudo joined the European Monetary System in April 1992 but it was obliged to devalue by 6 per cent later in the year and by a further 3.5 per cent in 1993. It devalued again by 3.5 per cent in 1995, remaining stable thereafter until becoming absorbed into the euro.

Portugal suffers from the lowest labour productivity in the EMU area. For the country as a whole, GDP per head is only 69 per cent of the EU average, which makes it the poorest of the EMU members and only slightly ahead of Greece (66.3 per cent).

Unemployment has had a tendency to remain quite low over a long period. It peaked at no higher than 8.7 per cent in the 1980s and has averaged below 7 per cent in the 1990s. Despite an apparently poor rate of internal migration, the regional dispersion of unemployment, which varies from 4.1 per cent to 8.9 per cent, is relatively low. Labour mobility to the rest of the EMU is higher than that of other countries. Thus the labour market does not suffer from the massive structural distortions of Spain and Italy.

The main problems for Portugal will be the lack of convergence of its economy with the rest of the EMU bloc and the low rate of labour productivity, which will severely hamper competitiveness.

IRELAND

Ireland has the smallest economy of the EMU participants, with a GDP only some 3 per cent that of Germany. As one of the poorer countries in the EU, Ireland has traditionally received a large net contribution from the EU budget, which still amounts to nearly 5 per cent of Irish GDP. However, this situation is now changing since by 1997 Irish GDP per capita had risen to 102.6 per cent of the EU average, compared with only 72 per cent in 1990.

In contrast to the rest of Europe, GDP growth accelerated during the 1990s, reaching an amazing 9 per cent *per annum* over the 1995–98 period. This was made possible by the reform of the government's finances which had threatened to get out of control in the 1980s, when the budget deficit was running at over 13 per cent of GDP. Tight budgets in the late 1980s served to bring government spending under control, resulting in lower inflation and interest rates, which in turn paved the way for the GDP growth miracle of the 1990s. Additional factors boosting GDP were the EU subsidies and an exceptionally good performance in productivity growth, easily the best of EMU participants. The strong expansion in GDP actually pushed the budget into surplus by 1997. Budgetary discipline also served to bring down the level of government debt from a peak of 114 per cent of GDP in 1987 to a more comfortable level of 53 per cent in 1998.

Ireland was one of Europe's high inflation economies until the mid-1980s. As a result of this the Irish pound, after joining the EMS in 1979, was forced to devalue regularly against the Deutschmark, by a total of around 35 per cent in the period to 1987 alone.

During the 1990s, as a result of the new economic policy, inflation was one of Europe's lowest. But by late 1998 the extended period of economic strength had brought the economy dangerously close to capacity constraints, with a tightening labour market. Having been for several years around 2 per cent or less, Irish inflation began to creep up again, reaching over 3 per cent, compared with an average for the EMU bloc of only 1.7 per cent.

It is clear, therefore, that the Irish economic cycle has been seriously out of line with the rest of the euro area. This was painfully apparent from the level of Irish short-term interest rates, which by the summer of 1998 were over 6 per cent, easily the highest of the euro countries. Irish rates were subsequently forced to decline sharply to the prevailing euro level by the end of the year – an inappropriate degree of monetary stimulation given the high level of economic activity.

A major factor helping Irish economic growth has been the strength of the UK economy in recent years. But the UK's reluctance to join EMU has created a major problem for Ireland, which is apparent from the breakdown of Irish trade. Trade with the UK is currently 30 per cent of the total, the same as for the whole of the euro area put together. It is true that Ireland is less tied to the UK than it used to be. Before joining the EC in 1973, the UK constituted some two-thirds of the total, and in 1986 it was still at 38 per cent, so the trend is clearly down. But given the high degree of openness in the Irish economy (exports total 74 per cent of GDP), the extent of the trade link with the UK means that the Irish economy will continue to be strongly influenced by the UK economic cycle.

The economy is particularly vulnerable to a fall in sterling against the euro, which by cutting Irish exports to the UK would cause a major dampening effect on the Irish economy, and one which would not be felt so strongly in the rest of the EMU area. This factor was reflected in the Irish pound's traditional sensitivity to sterling. After the latter's exit from the ERM in 1992 Ireland was obliged to follow with a 10 per cent devaluation in 1993. Following the strong recovery of sterling in the mid-1990s the Irish pound was drawn to the top of the ERM, as a result of which it was revalued by 3 per cent in March 1998. Now that the Irish pound effectively no longer exists this safety valve is removed.

Were sterling to join the EMU, of course the problem would be largely resolved and Irish trade with the euro area would then total 57 per cent.

A further problem with Ireland is that unemployment has been one of the highest in the EMU. Despite the years of very strong growth it was still well over 8 per cent in 1998. It is difficult to see labour mobility between Ireland and mainland Europe as a solution to this problem, since labour has always flowed to and from the UK due to proximity and cultural links. Around 15 per cent of the Irish population lives in the UK, whereas labour flows to the rest of Europe are minimal.

As a highly open economy, Ireland should in principle be an excellent candidate for monetary union but its trade structure is currently too biased towards non-EMU members. Further-

Ireland's trade structure is currently too biased towards non-EMU members.

more, it has joined EMU at the peak of its economic cycle, a totally different phase from that of the rest of the EMU bloc. As a small country on the periphery of the area, Ireland will have to adapt itself rapidly to the mainstream of events in the euro economy in order to survive.

Chapter 15

PROSPECTIVE EMU ENTRANTS

The question of enlargement has always been a difficult one for the EU. New members will undoubtedly wish to participate in EMU in the future, depending of course on how successful the venture actually is. Some countries from the former Eastern bloc may well eventually join the euro, either at the same time as or subsequent to entering the EU. This raises the question of the extent to which new members are suitable participants. To put this in perspective, we will discuss the four existing members of the EU who, for various reasons, have not joined the EMU at the start. These are Greece, who failed to qualify, and Denmark, Sweden and the UK, who all decided to remain outside for the time being. We will look at the structure of the economies concerned and discuss which of these four may be expected to join at a later date.

GREECE, DENMARK AND SWEDEN

Greece has been a member of the EU since as long ago as 1981. It has consistently remained the poorest member. Indeed, it is somewhat worrying that GDP per head, currently at around 66 per cent of the EU average, has barely improved since joining, having been 64 per cent of the average in 1981.

Greece has traditionally been an inflation-prone economy, averaging over 18 per cent in the 1980s, and as recently as 1994 the inflation rate was still at 11 per cent, more than three times the EU average. Since then government austerity policies have brought the rate down sharply to around 5 per cent. The budget deficit has been reduced from over 10 per cent a year in the first half of the 1990s to 4 per cent in 1997, and 2.4 per cent in 1998.

Trade flows are summarized in Table 15.1, from which it can be seen that trade with the EMU bloc represents a high proportion of the total at 55 per cent. This has been the case for many years – trade with member countries was over 50 per cent of the Greek total when the community was founded in 1958. Somewhat surprisingly for such a small country (only Portugal and Ireland in the EU are smaller) the Greek economy is not a particularly open one. The external sector constitutes only 16 per cent of GDP, much less than any other EU member, and the same level it was at in 1981. Membership of the Community thus cannot be said to have been trade-creating for Greece.

Table 15.1 Trade flows of prospective EMU members

Trade with	EMU bloc		Greece		Denmark		Sweden		UK	
	1986	1996	1986	1996	1986	1996	1986	1996	1986	1996
Greece	55.9	54.6			1.2	0.9	1.2	1.5	5.5	6.0
Denmark	43.0	44.4	0.6	0.4			11.8	10.9	9.5	7.8
Sweden	42.8	43.9	0.3	0.3	7.4	6.8			10.3	8.2
UK	49.6	47.0	0.5	0.4	1.9	1.2	3.2	2.4		

Average of exports and imports, per cent of total

Source: IMF *Direction of Trade* Yearbooks

GDP growth has begun to correlate more closely with the EMU bloc since the early 1990s, although it should be observed that some economic data may be unreliable due to the unrecorded size of the 'black' economy.

Regional disparities within Greece are not excessive, at least not by the standards of southern Europe, but productivity is uniformly low across all regions. Unemployment is not at the chronically high levels of Spain and southern Italy, but still varies from 4.4 per cent to 12 per cent across the regions. Labour flows from the rest of Europe into Greece are very low. On the positive side, a relatively high proportion of Greeks (over 3 per cent of the population) live and work elsewhere in the euro area, although this is the same level that prevailed in the late 1980s.

Financial markets are not as well developed as in the rest of the EMU, and short-term interest rates are still very high at 12 per cent. The drachma, traditionally a very weak currency, only joined the ERM in March 1998 but, supported by high interest rates, remained stable up to the start of EMU. The drachma remains linked to the euro as a member of the ERM but with a wide band of potential fluctuation.

Greece hoped, somewhat optimistically, to join EMU at the start but failed to achieve the requirements on budget deficit and inflation. The target is now to join in 2001. The feasibility of this date is highly questionable. Much depends on how EMU itself progresses over the intervening period, particularly with respect to the other southern European countries. The problem with Greece is that a long period of EU membership does not appear to have brought much in the way of economic convergence with its partners, particularly regarding trade and labour productivity. There are also major questions as to whether or not the required fiscal retrenchment can be sustained. The picture is one of a rather rudimentary economy, by European standards, which would have a good deal of trouble competing in the EMU bloc.

Denmark and Sweden, in contrast to Greece, passed the Maastricht criteria on inflation and government finances easily but in both cases opted not to enter EMU in the first round.

Denmark joined the EC in 1973. Trade flows with the EMU bloc stand at around 44 per cent of the total, little changed from ten years ago but up on pre-membership levels of 37 per cent. The

Danish krone participated in the Exchange Rate Mechanism from its outset in 1979, and in the early years of its membership was, as a relatively high inflation economy, forced to devalue several times. However, by the late 1980s inflation had been brought down to German levels, where it has remained ever since. The krone has thus been able to retain an unchanged Deutschmark parity in the ERM since 1986.

Rather surprisingly, Danish GDP growth correlates poorly with that of Germany, although the relationship has improved substantially since 1992. For several years unemployment (currently around 4 per cent) has been steadily declining while GDP has been growing comfortably, with the result that the government finances were in surplus by 1997. GDP per head at 116 per cent of the EU average is the highest in the Community (excluding Luxembourg).

Rather surprisingly, Danish GDP growth correlates poorly with that of Germany.

In general, Denmark would fit well into EMU, in common with the other small open economies on the periphery of Germany, i.e., Belgium, Austria and the Netherlands. Indeed most of the business community is in favour of joining, but there is a good deal of public scepticism. Much of the population is concerned that EMU will inevitably lead to political union in Europe. In late 1998 the government indicated that a referendum on the issue could be held before long. This statement reflected polls showing that public support for joining was now on the increase, although the government will doubtless wait until it is clear that a 'yes' vote is more or less guaranteed.

·Denmark is of course in a unique position because its exchange rate is tied to the euro on a narrow band, just as it was fixed against the Deutschmark for the previous 12 years. There is no particular reason for this parity to change, but as long as a separate currency exists, there is always the potential for exchange rate adjustment to occur. It seems probable, therefore, that this 'unofficial' member-ship of the euro will become complete within a year or two, as it becomes accepted by the public that life for Denmark will be eas-ier fully inside EMU.

Sweden is a different case from Denmark in that it never joined the ERM. Swedish experience of actual participation in European exchange rate arrangements is limited to a brief period in the Euro-pean currency 'snake' (the precursor of the ERM) in the 1970s. In 1991 the government announced that the krona would 'shadow' the ECU, but it was allowed to float again in 1993.

Things began to go badly wrong for the Swedish economy in the late 1980s. The extremely generous welfare state system, combined with an inefficient private sector overburdened with taxes, dragged the economy down. By the early 1990s government spending was approaching 70 per cent of GDP, with the budget deficit peaking at 12 per cent of GDP, and inflation at 10 per cent *per annum*. A series of austerity measures were implemented that involved the econ-omy contracting for three years in a row before recovering in 1994. Since then GDP has expanded steadily, and by 1998 inflation was around 1 per cent and the budget in surplus.

Economic activity has thus been somewhat volatile, and not the sort of harmonious convergence that would suggest a suitable EMU candidate. Regarding trade, 44 per cent of exports and imports are with the EMU bloc, plus another 7 per cent with the 'de facto' member Denmark. This fact, together with the large size of Swe-den's external sector (over 40 per cent of GDP) would suggest that the economy should increasingly move more in line with the euro area. Indeed, a closer correlation with the German economy has built up over the last few years. But the labour market remains somewhat inflexible and labour flows with the rest of Europe are minimal (other than with Finland). In terms of pure economics, the case for joining the euro would seem rather less favourable than that of Denmark.

Sweden joined the EU in 1995 and the decision to participate has not proved a particularly popular one. This dissatisfaction surfaced in the autumn 1998 general election, at which the anti-EU left-wing parties made a strong showing. But the Social Democratic government is apparently in favour of EMU, and has indicated that a referendum on the issue could be held before the next general election in 2002. To pave the way for membership, the government introduced measures in November 1998 to make the Central Bank politically independent, thus fulfilling one of the EMU requirements. At the same time opinion polls began to show the public more favourably disposed towards membership, although a large proportion of those questioned remained undecided. But the likely outcome of events is extremely uncertain, with major divisions across the political spectrum.

Sweden joined the EU in 1995 and the decision to participate has not proved a particularly popular one.

UNITED KINGDOM

The UK is an economy of an altogether different magnitude than the ones considered above, being five times the size of Sweden, and approximately the same size as France. Clearly, absorbing a major economy into the EMU is rather more problematical than absorbing a small one, given the potential for disrupting the harmony of the union. Thus it is even more crucial for a country the size of the UK that structural economic factors are clearly supportive of membership.

Regarding trade, just under 50 per cent of UK trade is conducted with EMU members, slightly down from ten years ago. This represents a considerable increase on the level of trade before the UK joined the EEC in 1973, when it ran at less than half the current proportion. The external sector constitutes around 27 per cent of the UK's GDP, so trade with the EMU represents about 13 per cent of GDP and trade outside the EMU the same. These are almost identical figures to those of the other large EMU members, Germany, France and Italy (*see* Table 13.7 on page 133). So, on a trade basis alone there would appear to be no disadvantages to UK membership.

However, other factors paint a somewhat different picture. In terms of the economic cycle, the UK has quite clearly pursued a path very different from the rest of Europe. This is confirmed by the UK Treasury's own analysis that accompanied Gordon Brown's EMU Statement of October 1997. Since 1979 the correlation of UK growth with that of Germany has been virtually zero, while the correlation with the US economy has been just over 0.5 (1.0 would represent a perfect correlation).

This lack of convergence reflects both policy and structural differences. On the policy side, monetary and fiscal decisions have generally been geared to objectives other than convergence with the rest of Europe, such as the British electoral cycle. When attempts to align the exchange rate with the Deutschmark have been made they have been short-lived and quickly blown off course by the vagaries of the UK economy. The first of these was the brief sterling membership of the European currency

In terms of the economic cycle, the UK has quite clearly pursued a path very different from the rest of Europe.

'snake' in 1972, which was terminated by the disastrous Heath–Barber boom. Secondly, there was the attempt to unofficially align sterling with the ERM by Chancellor Lawson in 1987–88. This resulted in an over-expansionary domestic monetary policy and consequent inflationary boom and bust. Finally, and most memorably, there was sterling's membership of the ERM beginning in October 1990. Sterling entered at too high an exchange rate, and one which was incompatible with the UK economic cycle, so that membership lasted less than two years before the currency was forced to leave in September 1992.

The UK economy differs from Europe structurally in important ways. First, it is a net exporter of oil, and is likely to remain so for the foreseeable future. Unlike the rest of Europe, the economy is vulnerable to large fluctuations in the oil price. In addition, the economy is generally more sensitive to movements in short-term interest rates. Much of this reflects the structure of the housing market. Owner-occupancy is high in the UK and is also primarily financed at variable interest rates. Treasury figures show that mortgage debt in the UK is 57 per cent of GDP compared with an EU average of only 33 per cent. This means that a given interest rate change would have much more effect in the UK than elsewhere in the euro area. So a monetary policy geared primarily to euro objectives would create a good deal of instability in the domestic economy.

In terms of the labour market, the UK is probably the most flexible economy in Europe. Internal interregional migration is, at least by European standards, high and the spread of regional unemployment relatively low. This is helped by less intrusive labour market regulations than elswhere. But labour flows with the rest of Europe are extremely small. Only 0.7 per cent of the population live elsewhere in the euro area, with annual migration at about 0.2 per cent. Similar figures apply regarding flows of labour to the UK from the EMU area (other than for Ireland, from where immigrants constitute 1 per cent of the UK population).

The economic case would thus argue against UK membership but, as with other countries, the outcome of events will probably be politically driven. Gordon Brown in his 1997 statement noted that, while the time was not yet right, British membership of EMU 'would be beneficial to Britain and to Europe' and that 'if a single currency works and is successful, Britain should join it'. The time frame suggested by Brown was 'early in the next Parliament', which would imply a referendum in 2001 or 2002. Further government statements in the course of 1998 confirmed that it was clearly supportive of membership, but the population at large has remained on balance against it, with memories of the 1992 ERM debacle still fresh. However, as these memories fade and as the government carefully paves the way with a 'pro' campaign, a referendum within the suggested time frame may well vote 'yes'. The fact that the government is in favour will be a strong plus, while political leadership of the 'anti' vote looks like remaining fractured. Certainly, pressure will be applied from the rest of the Union, since trade with the UK is a significant proportion of the total (around 8 per cent) for current EMU members. UK participation would thus cement the project further.

The economic case would thus argue against UK membership but the outcome of events will probably be politically driven.

The sheer volatility of sterling against the Deutschmark over the last 20 years would argue in favour of caution, and at least waiting for a modicum of economic convergence with Europe. But this would involve a much longer time frame than the present government is apparently prepared to countenance.

CONCLUSION

···

At midnight on 31 December 1998 the exchange rates of the participating members of EMU were locked into fixed parities. Thereafter, the ability of these countries to compete with each other is primarily a function of labour costs and productivity. The formation of a single currency area brings with it certain benefits, such as price transparency and a lowering of transaction costs. The European Commission has estimated that the implementation of the euro could represent a saving of around 0.5 per cent of the eurozone's overall GDP. As we have discussed, the loss of an individual exchange rate does, however, carry a cost in that it limits the policy options available to a country to deal with changing economic situations. Weighing up these benefits and costs, economic theory suggests that countries stand the best chance of forming a successful currency union if their economies are open, if they are similar in structure and are broadly in step with each other. It is also important to have a flexible and mobile labour market that can respond quickly to changing circumstances.

Our individual country analyses showed that, by virtue of their present trade structure and economic synchronization, there is a more natural 'pull' for some European countries to form a currency union than others.

Our individual country analyses showed that, by virtue of their present trade structure and economic synchronization, there is a more natural 'pull' for some European countries to form a currency union than others. On the basis of these observations, it is helpful to think of EMU in terms of an economic solar system.

Germany is at the heart of this system and, although it is experiencing some difficulties as a result of re-unification in 1990, it is

175

the dominant economy around which the rest of the EMU bloc must revolve.

The three smaller countries which orbit closest around the periphery of Germany are Austria, Belgium and the Netherlands. These countries qualify for EMU on both the trade structure and convergence counts and should experience fewer problems than the rest in adapting to a monetary union.

Just outside this inner circle is the major economic planet of France. In terms of optimum currency area theory, France's membership of EMU does not present any serious difficulties – even though its convergence with Germany is of a slightly more recent vintage than the countries in the inner core. The French economy is, of course, of a completely different order of magnitude to that of Austria, Belgium and the Netherlands and, if it were to pull in the opposite direction to that of Germany, it would create serious tensions in the system. But the degree of economic convergence has been such that, barring a major asymmetrical shock (caused, for example, by a radical change in government economic policy), this is unlikely to happen. The French labour market is, however, an area of concern since it is less efficient than that of Germany (excluding the eastern *Länder*) and the inner core countries but, providing measures are taken to reduce the present rigidities – and the political consensus for EMU holds – it should not be sufficient of a problem to jeopardize the whole project.

A little further out lie Ireland and Finland. In principle, these two small economies should be prime candidates for monetary union but their heavy dependence on trade with countries outside EMU does pose some risks. Ireland has very close trade links with the UK as Finland has with Sweden. Clearly, if the UK and Sweden were to join EMU, the problem would be solved but this remedy is still by no means certain.

Over time, Ireland and Finland's trade structure will shift towards their EMU partners, thereby justifying their participation, but it will only be a gradual transition and the Finnish economy will, for the foreseeable future, remain highly exposed to the forest products industry. In the meantime, both countries are still significantly 'out of step' economically with the main EMU bloc. A further problem is that there is very little in the way of labour mobility between either of these countries and the rest of the eurozone and, given their peripheral geographical location, it is questionable whether there will be any significant change in this situation for some time.

Portugal is another country that is currently on rather an outlying orbit. Its trade structure fits in well with EMU but, as a fairly recent recruit to the EU, its economic cycle has not yet had time to dovetail in with the rest of Europe. Given its small size and openness, this harmonization may not take too long to achieve and its labour market is more flexible than most. However, productivity is the lowest in the EMU and to compete effectively in the euro area the economy will need to improve its efficiency.

Right on the outside ring of the EMU solar system lie Italy and Spain. Although they score highly in terms of overall cyclical economic convergence, they suffer from by far the largest disparities in the levels of their regional unemployment. This is likely to prove to be a major problem for both these countries.

From an economic perspective therefore the biggest question mark hanging over EMU is the state of the European labour market. The combination of high levels of social security payments, relatively high minimum wages and, in some countries, strong trade unions has produced an inflexible work force which is unable to respond quickly to changing economic conditions and new technologies. Clearly, if people are reluctant to move from one area to another within one country to find work, they are likely to be even more unwilling to cross national boundaries where they will face additional linguistic and cultural barriers.

It is interesting that in both the US and the UK, where the labour markets are much more flexible, rapid job creation in the 1990s has resulted in significantly lower unemployment levels than in Europe. In the case of the US, a total of 12.5 million new jobs have been created since 1990 whereas in continental Europe there has been no net increase. Trying to pinpoint the exact cause of this 'Eurosclerosis' is a matter of great debate. Some economists, for example, believe that inefficient capital markets are at the root of the problem. But it is hard to believe that Europe's very much more rigid labour markets are not to a large extent responsible for the widely divergent trends seen in the US and continental Europe. Deregulation and reducing non-wage costs would therefore inject some dynamism into Europe's sluggish private sector.

The experience of the currency union between East and West Germany shows clearly the error of trying to harmonize wage rates while there is a large disparity in productivity levels. A rise in wage costs in regions of low productivity would only lead to redundancies in what are, for the most part, already areas of high unemployment.

Given Europe's structural problems, it is unfortunate that additional pressures may be brought to bear on the labour market in the early years of monetary union. A single currency will make for more transparent pricing, transforming the EMU area into a truly single market. This is likely to lead to a radical restructuring of the European corporate sector. Although in the long term this will make it better able to compete with the other major trading blocs, the initial rationalization process could result in a rise in the overall level of unemployment in the EU.

In the past rising unemployment has accentuated regional disparities. If unemployment continues to mount in the poor uncompetitive regions of the eurozone, there will be pressure on the relevant governments to increase fiscal spending (the only policy tool now at their disposal). However, the tightly drawn constraints of the stability pact leave little head-room for fiscal expansion dur-

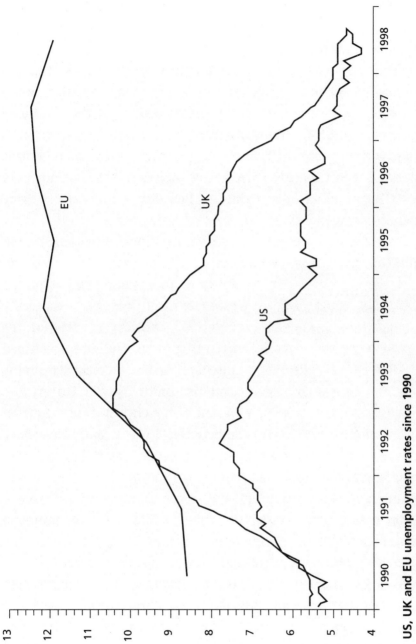

US, UK and EU unemployment rates since 1990

Source: Datastream/ICV

ing an economic downturn. The only way out of this predicament would be either to relax the stability pact or to develop a more centralized fiscal system that might eventually be a precursor to some form of political union.

Our analysis of past currency unions tends to suggest that economic forces alone are seldom sufficient to hold a monetary union together for a sustained period; there needs to be the additional glue of a political union. However, the difficulty experienced in ratifying the Maastricht Treaty suggests that there would be little public support for any steps in this direction – at least not until EMU has had sufficient time to bed down and deliver some tangible benefits.

Political dynamics have played an extremely important part in the construction of policies designed to achieve closer European integration. It is never wise to underestimate the risk of war – especially given the military confrontations occurring in Eastern Europe between the states that have emerged from the collapse of the Soviet Union and Yugoslavia – but, largely as a result of the efforts of the European integrationists, the risks of war between Germany and France have receded. The political dimension of EMU may now shift from balancing power between states to the *vox populi*. The concept of economic and monetary union has never commanded widespread support amongst the European electorate and, if it were to come to be associated in the electorate's mind with rising unemployment, there could be a severe political backlash against the idea.

Economic forces alone are seldom sufficient to hold a monetary union together for a sustained period.

Trying to steer this vast and unwieldy economic solar system through the financial universe is the European Central Bank. Clearly a major determinant of the overall success of EMU will be how successful the ECB is at piloting a smooth monetary course and avoiding too many jarring bumps along the way. Their task may be made more difficult by the changes that have occurred in Europe's political landscape. With so many governments now espousing Keynesian-style economic policies, this could bring them into conflict with the ECB's more monetarist leanings.

The ECB's primary responsibility is to ensure price stability and cohesion within its own system but the creation of the euro will have a very significant impact on the rest of the global markets. As the combined GDP of the 11 euro countries is only slightly smaller than that of the US, the euro will become a major global currency and could eventually usurp the dollar's role as the international unit of account. There is, however, one very marked difference between the dollar and the euro; the former is the currency of a sovereign state while the latter is not. The IMF has drawn attention to the ambiguity surrounding where exactly the role of lender of last resort is assigned for the euro. Therefore, before it can begin to challenge the dollar's dominance, the euro will need to establish credibility with the capital markets. Investors will need to be convinced that the EU will remain a cohesive monetary union before switching out of dollars into euro-dominated instruments on a large scale. The euro will also have to build up its volume of turnover to a level whereby its transaction costs can match those of the dollar. The emergence of a second 'reserve currency' – a role which neither the Deutschmark or yen have really fulfilled – is likely to increase competition in the financial markets and therefore have a beneficial effect.

Europe's capital markets are likely to undergo a radical change, becoming much more like their US counterpart. European companies which, in the past, have tended to rely on bank financing are likely to increasingly tap the markets directly for capital. As these markets become deeper and more liquid, the cost of raising capital is likely to fall. The capital markets are likely to reflect changes in the corporate sector – with more emphasis being placed on pan-European sectors rather than individual countries.

The euro's international role also raises other political issues. Henry Kissinger, the US Secretary of State from 1973 to 1977, once reportedly asked, 'If I want to speak to Europe, whom do I call?' (Echikson, 1997). As the EU is not a sovereign state, it will not be represented *per se* on international bodies such as the IMF and at G-7 meetings, although the president of the European Commission is allowed 'fly-on-the-wall' status. There is already a feeling among some countries that Europe is over-represented in the international arena and the lack of any single political representative of the euro may prompt a re-examination of the composition of some international organizations.

The lack of any single political representative of the euro may prompt a re-examination of the composition of some international organizations.

In the past 50 years the face of Europe has undergone a remarkable transformation. The scars of the Second World War have healed and, in the process, a strong and powerful trading bloc has emerged. It is a natural progression to try and extend this relationship to economic and monetary union but this does pose considerable political and economic challenges. The most immediate of these is a radical shake-up of Europe's labour markets and probably also a modification of the rules regarding fiscal policy. If these are carried out, the new economic solar system will be well placed to survive the first half of the twenty-first century and to assimilate new recruits. Failure to make sufficiently far-reaching changes is likely to result in a shrinking of the system as countries on the outlying orbits gradually drop away.

BIBLIOGRAPHY

Ardagh, J. (1982) *France in the 1980s*. Harmondsworth: Penguin Books.

Ardagh, J. (1995) *Germany and the Germans*. Harmondsworth: Penguin Books.

Artis, M. and Winkler, B. (1997) *The Stability Pact: Safeguarding the Credibility of the European Central Bank*. London: Centre for Economic Policy Research.

Artis, M. and Zhang, W. (1995) *International Business Cycles and the ERM: Is There a European Business Cycle?*. London: Centre for Economic Policy Research.

Bayoumi, T. and Eichengreen, B. (1996) *Operationalizing the Theory of Optimum Currency Areas*. London: Centre for Economic Policy Research.

Bayoumi, T. and Masson, P. (1994) *Fiscal Flows in the United States and Canada: Lessons for Monetary Union in Europe*. London: Centre for Economic Policy Research.

Bayoumi, T. and Prasad, E. (1995) *Currency Unions, Economic Fluctuations and Adjustment: Some Empirical Evidence*. London: Centre for Economic Policy Research.

Bertola, G. (1989) 'Factor mobility, uncertainty and exchange rate regimes' in de Cecco, M. and Giovanni, A. *A European Central Bank?* Cambridge: Cambridge University Press.

Bofinger, P. (1994). *Is Europe an Optimum Currency Area?* London: Centre for Economic Policy Research.

de Cecco, M. and Giovanni, A. (1989) 'Does Europe need its own central bank?' in de Cecco, M. and Giovanni, A. *A European Central Bank?* Cambridge: Cambridge University Press.

Centre for Economic Policy Research (1995) *Unemployment: Choices for Europe*. London: Centre for Economic Policy Research.

Cohen, B. J. (1993) 'Beyond EMU: the problem of sustainability' in Eichengreen, B. and Frieden, J. *The Political Economy of European Monetary Integration*. Boulder: Westview Press.

Colchester, N. and Buchan, D. (1990) *Europe Relaunched, Truths and Illusions on the Way to 1992*. London: Hutchinson Business Books.

Cox, S. (1992) *A Development of the European Community*. University of Huddersfield.

Davies, N. (1997) *Europe: a history*. London: Pimlico.

Delors Committee (1989) *Report on Economic and Monetary Union in the European Community*. Luxembourg.

Dornbusch, R. (1976) 'Expectations and exchange rate dynamics' in *Journal of Political Economy*, December.

Echikson, W. (1997) *Business Weekly*, 5 May.

Economist Intelligence Unit (1997–8) *Country Profile. 1997–98.*

Eichengreen, B. (1992) 'Designing a central bank for Europe: a cautionary tale from the early years of the Federal Reserve System' in Canzoni, M., Grilli, V. and Masson, P. *Establishing a Central Bank: Issues in Europe and Lessons from the United States.* Cambridge: Cambridge University Press.

Eichengreen, B. (1993) 'Labor markets and European monetary unification' in Masson, P. and Taylor, M. *Policy Issues in the Operation of Currency Unions.* Cambridge: Cambridge University Press.

Eichengreen, B. and von Hagan, J. (1995) *Fiscal Policy and Monetary Union: Federalism, Fiscal Restrictions and the No-Bailout rule.* London: Centre for Economic Policy Research.

European Commission (1977) *Report of the Study Group on the Role of Public Finance in European Integration.* Brussels.

Fatas, A. (1998) *Redistribution vs Insurance: Does Europe Need a Fiscal Federation?* London: Centre for Economic Policy Research.

Frankel, J. and Rose, A. (1996) *The Endogeneity of the Optimum Currency Area Criteria.* London: Centre for Economic Policy Research.

Friedman, M. (1968) 'The role of monetary policy' in *American Economic Review*, vol 58.

Gilbert, M. (1988) *Never Despair: Winston S. Churchill 1945–65.* London: Heinemann.

de Grauwe, P. (1997) *The Economics of Monetary Integration.* Oxford: Oxford University Press.

de Grauwe, P. and Vanhaverbeke, W. (1993) 'Is Europe an optimum currency area: evidence from the regional data' in Masson, P. and Taylor, M. *Policy Issues in the Operation of Currency Unions.* Cambridge: Cambridge University Press.

Holtfrerich, C-L. (1989) 'The monetary unification process in nineteenth-century Germany: relevance and lessons for Europe today' in de Cecco, M. and Giovanni, A. *A European Central Bank.* Cambridge: Cambridge University Press.

Honohan, P. (1994) *Currency Board or Central Bank? Lessons from the Irish Pound's Link with Sterling, 1928–79.* London: Centre for Economic Policy Research.

IMF *Direction of Trade* Yearbooks.

Johnson, H. G. (1969) 'The "Problems" approach to international monetary reform' in Mundell, R. A. and Swoboda, A. K. *Monetary Problems of the International Economy.* Chicago: University of Chicago Press.

Kenen, P. B. (1969) 'The theory of optimum currency areas: an eclectic view' in Mundell, R. A. and Swoboda, A. K. *Monetary Problems of the International Economy*. Chicago: University of Chicago Press.

Keynes, John Maynard (1919) *The Economic Consequences of Peace*. London: Macmillan & Co.

Laughland, J. (1991) 'European Union the German way' *Spectator*, 30 November.

Laughland, J. (1993) 'Power is without responsibility' *Spectator*, 17 July.

Leonard, D. (1993) *The Economist's Guide to the European Community*. London: Century.

Masson, P. and Taylor, M. (1993) 'Currency unions: a survey of the issues' in Masson, P. and Taylor, M. *Policy Issues in the Operation of Currency Unions*. Cambridge: Cambridge University Press.

McCallum, J. (1997) 'A Canadian lesson for EMU' in *Wall Street Journal*, 16 December.

McKinnon, R. I. (1963) 'Optimum currency areas' in *American Economic Review*, Vol. 53.

Miron, J. A. (1989) 'The founding of the Fed and the destabilization of the post-1914 economy' in de Cecco, M. and Giovanni, A. *A European Central Bank?*. Cambridge: Cambridge University Press.

Mundell, R. A. (1961) 'A theory of optimum currency areas' in *American Economic Review*, Vol. 51.

OECD (1994) *The OECD Jobs Study: Facts, Analysis, Strategies*. Paris.

OECD (1997) *Economic Outlook*. December, Paris.

Phelps, E. S. (1970) 'Money wage dynamics and labor market equilibrium' in Phelps, E. S. (ed.) (1971) *Microeconomic Foundations of Employment and Inflation Theory*. New York: Norton.

Redish, A. (1993) 'The Latin monetary union and the emergence of the gold standard' in Bordo, M. and Capie, F. *Monetary Regimes in Transition*. Cambridge: Cambridge University Press.

Robertson, A. H. (1956) *The Council of Europe: Its Structures and Functions and Achievements*. London Institute of World Affairs and London: Stevens & Sons.

Sala-i-Martin, X. and Sachs, J. (1992) 'Fiscal federalism and optimum currency areas: evidence for Europe from the United States' in Canzoneri, M. Grilli, V. and Masson, P. *Establishing a Central Bank*. Cambridge: Cambridge University Press.

Sannucci, V. (1989) 'The establishment of a central bank: Italy in the nineteenth century' in de Cecco, M. and Giovanni, A. *A European Central Bank?*. Cambridge: Cambridge University Press.

Tavlas, G. S. (1993) 'The "New" theories of optimum currency areas' in *The World Economy*, Vol. 16.

Taylor, A. J. P. (1971) *The Struggle for Mastery in Europe 1848–1918*. Oxford: Oxford University Press.

Thomson, D. (1967) *Europe Since Napoleon*. Harmondsworth: Pelican Books.

Urwin, D. (1991) *The Community of Europe*. London: Longman.

Vanthoor, W. (1996) *European Monetary Union since 1848*. Cheltenham: Elgar.

Willis, F. R. (1969) *France, Germany and the New Europe 1945–1976*. Oxford: Oxford University Press.

Wilson, Woodrow (1927) *War and Peace, Presidential Messages, Addresses and Public Papers (1917–1924)*. Edited by R. S. Baker and W. E. Dodd. New York and London: Harper & Brothers.

INDEX

Adenauer, Chancellor 27, 41
Alberta 135
Alsace 6, 8, 9
Artis, M. 117
asset market approach to currencies 86
asymmetrical shocks 102–3
Austria 29, 156–7, 176
Austrian/German monetary union 54–5
Austrian/Hungarian monetary union 55

balance of power 3–4
Barre, Raymond 143
Bayoumi, T. 118
Belgium 154–5, 176
Belgium–Luxembourg economic union 55–7
Bertola, G. 80
Bofinger, P. 86
Bretton Woods system 29
Britain see United Kingdom
Brussels, Treaty of 19, 21
budget deficits 109–10, 112
    stability pact 113–18
Bundesbank 97–8

Canada
    economic diversification 134–5
    fiscal policy 118, 119, 120
    labour mobility 128–30
capital markets 181
centralization of fiscal policy 110–11
CFA franc see Franc des Colonies Françaises d'Afrique
Churchill, Winston xiii
closed economies 71–5, 81

coal and steel industry 4, 5, 11, 14–15, 18–19
Common Agricultural Policy 25
Common Assembly 18
costs of separate currencies 86
Council of Europe 17–18
Council of Ministers 18, 22
Court of Justice 18, 19, 22
'currency board' system 66
currency markets see foreign exchange markets

Davies, N. 9, 13
Davignon, Étienne 28
Delors, Jacques 31
Delors Report 34–5, 107–8
Denmark 38, 53, 167–9
devaluations 87–8
diversification 75–6, 77, 84–5, 134–5
Dooge, James 34
Dornbusch, R. 86
Dublin summit 35
Duisenberg, Wim 101

East African Currency Union 58
East Caribbean Currency Area 58
economic convergence 85, 93, 134–8
economic cycle 136–8
economic diversification 75–6, 77, 84–5, 134–5
ECU (European Currency Unit) 30
EDC (European Defence Community) 20
Eden, Anthony 21
EEC see European Economic Community
EFTA see European Free Trade Area
Eichengreen, B. 118, 119, 127

EMI *see* European Monetary Institute
EMS *see* European Monetary System
Erhard, Ludwig 27, 41
ERM *see* Exchange Rate Mechanism
euro 39
European Assembly 22
European Atomic Energy
    Community (Euratom) 22, 23
European Central Bank (ECB) 37,
    97–102, 180–1
  goal of 100
  independence guarantees 104
  as lender of last resort 99–100
  monetary targeting 100–1
  structure 98–9
European Coal and Steel
    Community 11, 14–15, 18–19
European Commission 22
European Council 22
European Currency Unit (ECU) 30
European Defence Community
    (EDC) 20
European Economic Community
    (EEC) xiii, 22
  budgetary crisis 31, 33–4
  enlargement 29
European Free Trade Area (EFTA)
    26
European Monetary Institute (EMI)
    37
European Monetary System (EMS)
    30–1
European System of Central Banks
    37, 52, 99
European unit of account (EUA)
    30
Exchange Rate Mechanism (ERM)
    30–1, 38–9, 87, 148, 163
exchange rates as policy tool 72, 74,
    87–8

factor mobility 67–71, 77, 79–80
  and flexible labour markets 67–9,
    80

and inflexible labour markets
  69–71, 80
labour mobility 80, 92
and wages 79–80
Fatas, A. 118
federal fiscal policy 110–11
Federal Open Market Committee
  (FOMC) 51
Federal Reserve 51–2
Finland 29, 137, 157–60, 176–7
First World War 6–7
fiscal policy xvii, 107–20
  Belgium 155
  budget deficits 109–10, 112
  Canada 118, 119, 120
  centralization of 110–11
  Delors report 107–8
  effectiveness of 108
  Finland 159
  under fixed exchange rates 109
  Ireland 162
  Maastricht criteria 111–12
  and monetary policy 98, 101
  openness of economies 108–9
  stability pact 113–18
  United States 118, 119
fixed exchange rates 66, 109
flexible labour markets 67–9, 80
floating exchange rates 66
FOMC *see* Federal Open Market
  Committee
Fontainbleau summit 33
foreign exchange markets 85–8
  asset market approach to
    currencies 86
  costs of separate currencies 86
  devaluations 87–8
  exchange rates as policy tool 72,
    74, 87–8
  fixed exchange rates 66, 109
  floating exchange rates 66
  volatility of currencies 86–7
Franc des Colonies Françaises
    d'Afrique (CFA) 58

franc fort policy 143
France 3–9, 142–7, 176
    coal and steel production 4, 5
    'empty chair' policy 27–8
    exports 81
    foreign policy 8
    Franco-German co-operation
        treaty 27
    Franco-Prussian war 3, 4, 6
    inflation 143
    labour market 176
    Latin Monetary Union 52–3
    Maastricht Treaty ratification 38
    and NATO 28
    Saar dispute 13–14
    unemployment 146
    Vichy government 9
Franco-German co-operation treaty
    27
Franco-Prussian war 3, 4, 6
Frankfurt, Treaty of 4, 6

Gaulle, Charles de 25–7, 28
German/Austrian monetary union
    54–5
Germany 3–9, 139–42, 175–6
    coal and steel production 4, 5
    customs union (*Zollverein*) xiv, 48
    economic cycle 136–7
    expansionary ambitions 6
    Franco-German co-operation
        treaty 27
    Franco-Prussian war 3, 4, 6
    Maastricht Treaty ratification 38
    military occupation 12
    and NATO 43
    political unification (1834–71)
        48–50
    and political union 42–4
    productivity 135–6
    re-unification 36, 42, 58–60,
        139–40, 141
    Reichsbank 49
    reparation payments 7

Saar dispute 13–14
    unemployment 125, 140
gold standard 55
Greece 26, 29, 165–7

Hague summit 28
Hanover summit 34
High Authority (of ECSC) 18
Hitler, Adolf 8–9
Hungarian/Austrian monetary union
    55

inflation 81–4
    convergence of 75, 77, 81
    in France 143
    in Ireland 162–3
    in Italy 88–9, 147–8
    and money supply 100
    in Spain 150
    and unemployment 81–3
inflexible labour markets 69–71, 80,
    130–2
interest rates 103
Ireland 162–4
    fiscal policy 162
    inflation 162
    monetary union with Britain 57
    trade structure 133–4, 137, 138,
        176–7
Israel 26
Italy 147–9
    budget deficit 110
    exports 81
    fiscal control 148–9
    formation of 47
    inflation 88–9, 147–8
    monetary union 47–8
    productivity 135–6
    unemployment 125, 149

Jenkins, Roy 30
Johnson, Harry 77

Kenen, P.B. 75, 107

Kenya 58
Keynes, John Maynard 7
Kohl, Helmut 42–3, 44
Korean War 17, 19

labour markets 123–6, 177–8
    flexible 67–9, 80
    France 176
    Germany 59–60
    inflexible 69–71, 80, 130–2
    Spain 151
    United States 59–60, 126–8, 177–8
    wages 79–80
labour mobility 80, 92, 128–30
Latin Monetary Union (LMU) 52–3
Lorraine 6, 8, 9
Lubbers, Ruud 152
Luxembourg Compromise 28
Luxembourg summit 34
Luxembourg–Belgium economic
    union 55–7

Maastricht Treaty 36–7
    convergence criteria 93
    fiscal policy criteria 111–12
    ratification 38
McCallum, J. 130, 135
MacDougall Report 107
McKinnon, R.I. 71
Major, John 36
Marshall Plan 11, 12–13
Masson, P. 118
military policy 17
    European Defence Community
        (EDC) 20
    North Atlantic Treaty
        Organization (NATO) 19, 21, 28,
        43
minimum wage 131
Mitterand, François 33, 42
monetary policy xv, 29–30, 97–105
    asymmetrical shocks 102–3
    European Monetary System (EMS)
        30–1

    and fiscal policy 98, 101
    political conflict 104
    'snake' 29, 30
    transmission mechanisms 103–4
monetary targeting 100–1
monetary union
    advantages 66–7, 91–2
    Hague summit 28
    preceded by political union 60
    transitional period 39
money supply 100
Monnet, Jean 14
Mundell, Robert 65

Netherlands 125, 152–3, 176
North Atlantic Treaty Organization
    (NATO) 19, 21, 28, 43
Norway 29, 53

open economies 71–5, 77, 81, 92–3
    and fiscal policy 108–9
    and trade structure 132–4
optimum currency area theory
    xiv–xv, 65–77
    advantages of monetary union
        66–7, 91–2
    economic diversification 75–6, 77,
        84–5
    factor mobility 67–71, 77, 79–80
    inflation rates 75, 77, 81–4
    openness of economies 71–5, 77,
        81, 92–3
Organization for European
    Economic Co-operation (OEEC)
    13

Paris Accords 21
Paris, Treaty of 18
Parliamentary Assembly 22
Pleven Plan 20
political integration 17–18
political union 28, 41–4
    preceding monetary union 60
Pompidou, Georges 28

Portugal 29, 125, 160–1, 177
Potsdam conference 19
productivity 59–60, 135–6

Reichsbank 49
reparation payments 7
Robertson, A.H. 18
Rome, Treaty of 21–3

Saar dispute 13–14
Scandinavian monetary union 53–4
Schuman Plan 14–15
Second World War 8–9
single currency 37
Single European Act 34
'snake' 29, 30
Spaak, Paul-Henri 22, 41
Spain 29, 150–1
stability pact 113–18
steel and coal industry 4, 5, 11,
    14–15, 18–19
Strasbourg summit 35
Sweden 29, 53, 137–8, 169–70, 176

Tanzania 58
Tavlas, G.S. 88
Taylor, A.J.P. 6
Texas 71, 103
Thatcher, Margaret 31, 34
Thomson, D. 13
trade structure 132–4
transmission of monetary policy
    103–4
Triple Alliance 6
Triple Entente 6
Turkey 26

Uganda 58
unemployment 123–7, 178–9
    Austria 157
    Finland 159
    France 146

Germany 140
    and inflation 81–3
    Italy 149
    Netherlands 153
    Portugal 161
    Spain 151
    United States 126–7
    unemployment benefits 130–1
    United Kingdom 170–3
    budget contributions 31, 33
    coal and steel production 5
    EEC membership 26–9
    Irish monetary union 57
    labour market 177–8
    Maastricht Treaty ratification 38
United States
    economic stabilization 118
    Federal Open Market Committee
        (FOMC) 51
    Federal Reserve 51–2
    fiscal policy 118, 119
    industry shocks 102
    labour market 59–60, 126–8,
        177–8
    monetary union 50–2
    unemployment 126–7

Vichy government 9
volatility of currencies 86–7
von Hagen, J. 118, 119

wages 59, 79–80, 131
Werner, Pierre 28
Werner report 29
Western Europe Union 21
Willis, F.R. 14, 20, 21, 26, 27
Wilson, Woodrow 7
Winkler, B. 117

Yalta conference 19

Zollverein xiv, 48